Hey Doc!
Does Speling Count?

A Satire About the Decline of
Higher Education in America

by
William W. Ward, Ph.D.
Illustrated by Lori Baratta

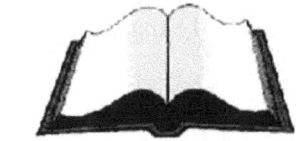

CCB Publishing
British Columbia, Canada

Hey Doc! Does Speling Count?: A Satire About the Decline of Higher Education in America

Copyright ©2008 by William W. Ward
ISBN-13   978-1-926585-02-4
First Edition

Library and Archives Canada Cataloguing in Publication

Ward, William W. (William Warren), 1942-
Hey Doc! Does speling [sic] count?: a satire about the decline of higher education in America / written by William W. Ward; illustrated by Lori Baratta.
Includes index.
ISBN 978-1-926585-02-4
1. State universities and colleges--United States--Humor. 2. Education, Higher--United States--Humor. 3. College students--United States--Humor. 4. Satire, American. I. Title. II. Title: Hey Doc! Does spelling count.
PN6231.C6W37 2008   813'.6   C2008-906227-2

Illustrator: Lori Baratta
Editor: Randy Ward

Extreme care has been taken to ensure that all information presented in this book is accurate and up to date at the time of publishing. Neither the author nor the publisher can be held responsible for any errors or omissions. Additionally, neither is any liability assumed for damages resulting from the use of the information contained herein.

All rights reserved. No part of this publication may be reproduced, stored in a retrieval system or transmitted in any form or by any means, electronic, mechanical, photocopying, recording or otherwise without the express written permission of the publisher. Printed in the United States of America and the United Kingdom.

Publisher: CCB Publishing
             British Columbia, Canada
             www.ccbpublishing.com

I dedicate this book to my parents, Frank and Betty Ward, exceptional people who have always been there for me. While a loving father in his own way, Dad never seemed satisfied with my personal accomplishments or my "one-track mind." Mom, on the other hand, has always been unconditionally supportive. I remember my final report card in 9th grade—29 A's and 1 lonely B in the upper left hand corner. True to form, Mom bragged about my grades to everyone while Dad just asked, "Hey! What's with the B?" Dad died in an automobile accident 14 years ago, but I still struggle every day to meet his expectations. Mom, still alert and quite self sufficient at 93, is the source of strength for the entire family.

Contents

Introduction vii

Foreword xi

Section I
Pre-College Knowledge

Chapter 1: Hector's Hints on Picking a Real Good College 1

Chapter 2: Private vs. Public – So Many Choices 9

Chapter 3: Hector's Basic Training (You Gotta Start Early) 13

Section II
So You've Chosen State U., My Alma Mater

Chapter 4: Hector's History of State U. 33

Chapter 5: Endless Adjustments 48

Section III
Off to a Real Good Start

Chapter 6: Choosing a Computer 59

Chapter 7: Hector's Hints to get in Real Good with
Your Professors 68

Chapter 8: Modular Answers to Test Questions 71

Chapter 9: Beating the M/C System 75

Chapter 10: Origin of the Grading Curve 81

Chapter 11: The University Presidents'
Standard Grading Curve 87

Section IV
Your Later College Years

Chapter 12:	How to Do Real Good Lab Reports for Your TA	95
Chapter 13:	Doing Graphs in College	103
Chapter 14:	Hector's Advice for Pre-Med Students	113
Chapter 15:	The Effortless Honors Project	117
Chapter 16:	Choosing a Major	125
Chapter 17:	Hector's Graduation Tips	130

Section V
They Put Me On the State U. Board? I Can't Believe it!

Chapter 18:	Heads Up On the Administration	143
Chapter 19:	The University as a Tax-Supported Minor League for the NFL and NBA	154
Chapter 20:	State U. Incorporated	165
Chapter 21:	How Universities Govern Themselves	177

Appendix 195

Index 200

INTRODUCTION

Hey, Doc! Does Speling Count? is a satire about the decline of higher education in state universities throughout the US. The setting is a hypothetical state university called State U. In the tradition of true satirical prose, I advance a serious message for mature readers using exaggeration coupled with politically incorrect humor. No one, from student to professor to university president to faculty union, escapes my lampooning. I direct plenty of heat at multiple-choice exams, the substitution of computer software for student gray matter, pre-med students, grade inflation, university governance (or what's left thereof), intercollegiate athletics, university attorneys, and self-serving, power-hungry university administrators. Especially hard hit are the State U. Governing Board and numerous corporations freely feeding at the State U. trough.

I wrote this book to focus attention on the problems in higher education -- particularly at state universities. I address serious problems, not the least of which is an extraordinarily lack of institutional emphasis on meaningful teaching and effective learning.

In general, we do a poor job of college teaching. We graduate students lacking the general skills they need to cope adequately in today's complex society. Even in scientific or technical fields, our students graduate without the tools they need to move effectively into the workforce or into post-graduate professional schools.

"Successful" students learn to memorize meaningless facts and to parrot them back via equally meaningless, computer-graded, multiple-choice exams. Never in the history of education, has memorizing facts and parroting them back been so irrelevant. Never before has society so demanded its college-educated citizenry to integrate knowledge. Never before have in-depth understanding and excellent communication skills been so important.

Today's students have more access to facts than any generation in the history of civilization. They don't need more facts. Yet, in lecture format, we deliver disjointed facts and then reward simple, short-term memorization of those facts. We continue this form of teaching at the exclusion of methods involving deeper understanding, conversational knowledge, and ability to write coherently.

Students run "data circles" around their professors as they acquire countless facts over the Internet. Yet, they have rudimentary ability to integrate knowledge and to effectively communicate their understanding of knowledge.

Most college students cannot think, write, or solve problems. We, as professors, do little to help them develop their thinking, writing, and problem-solving skills. Students in my Introductory Biochemistry Laboratory classes are unable to utilize what they supposedly learned in General Chemistry, General Biology, Organic Chemistry, Calculus, Physics, and a host of science electives. Not once, in thirty years of college teaching, for example, have I found a student who can observe a faucet aspirator and figure out how it draws a vacuum. Not once has a student said, "Oh! I learned that in physics class. Isn't that based on the Bernoulli Principle?" Not once in thirty years has my careful analogy to wing lift in airplane flight stimulated the slightest spark of insight on the workings of a faucet aspirator. Each is an example of fluid dynamics as described by the Bernoulli Principle. But, my students can't explain either example and they can't see the common principle uniting the two. Each student draws a blank.

If I want to teach any science to my junior/senior level biochemistry students, (how an overhead fluorescent lamp operates, what happens to egg white when you beat it, or how Darwinian concepts of evolution are repeated at the molecular level), I must first re-teach General Chemistry, General Biology, Organic Chemistry, Calculus, and Physics. Whatever students may remember from these prerequisite courses, they are incapable of using it in conversation, in quizzes, and in problem-solving exercises of any sort.

The fault lies not with the students. They are innocent victims of a failing educational system. Not even the professors can be blamed. The root of the problem lies within the social structure and value system of higher education administrators. Top university administrators are out of touch with what's happening in the classroom. It's not benign neglect isolating them from sound educational philosophy and practice. The fact of the matter is that senior administrators don't care to be in touch with classroom activities. College teaching, no matter how essential, no matter how outstanding, and no matter how innovative, is not on their radar screens.

Instead, top college administrators are preoccupied with running a business they pretend to own. As "private owners" of the state university, they make huge monetary investments (of taxpayers dollars) in intercollegiate sports. Obsession with college football is their primary strategy for showing off a business they unilaterally control. While there is an important relationship between teaching and the generation of tuition dollars, teaching brings no overhead money and does nothing to advance a top administrator's corporate stature. It's expected that college administrators will support the teaching program, but they would rather not bother. They want warm bodies (or cyber professors) to show up on a regular basis at the classroom podium. This ensures a steady stream of tuition dollars, providing a stable economic basis for their other interests. They cater to needs of the state's private corporations in attracting further resources, some of which wind up in the pockets of the top administrators.

This administrative attitude of irresponsible indifference filters down to the professors. Newly hired professors learn one fact very quickly -- teaching counts for nothing at the state university. In fact, their tenured colleagues carefully instruct them to avoid classroom teaching for the first six years so they can build a competitive, income-generating research program and a stellar record of grantsmanship. Bringing in money from external granting agencies is what counts -- several million dollars per year with huge overheads grabbed by the administration. Then, having survived six years of brainwashing, promoted professors unwittingly continue the pattern of raising grant money, writing research papers, and showing up to teach a few uninspiring lectures -- because some teaching is expected of most professors.

Our system of higher education is a sinking ship. And the captain of that ship is the top university administrator, ordering full steam ahead, despite a gaping hole in the structure.

This satire is meant to entertain, amuse, and stimulate while offering a serious message to receptive readers. By no means is this a factual exposé. No names are given; no institution is singled out. Read the book for pleasure while reflecting, to the extent you wish, on its deeper meaning.

I tell my story through a fictitious narrator, Hector, a lovable buffoon who is neither smart nor talented. Some years ago, he slipped though State U., ranking last in his class. Nonetheless, he landed a job with a six-figure salary and was invited to sit on State U's Board of Governors. Combining his personal history as a State U. student with his newer experiences as a State U. administrator, Hector writes a "how-to" book for college-bound students.

He describes how easy it is for young people to get through college. Deferring to Cliff, a smarter but less principled father figure, Hector frequently expresses Cliff's more reactionary points of view and involuntarily "borrows" Cliff's more sophisticated wording. Hector does this with little or no comprehension.

Narration by an undeserving character who has stumbled into a position of university leadership is satirical in its own right. According to Hector, it's all in knowing the tricks.

William W. Ward, PhD

FOREWORD

Hi! My name is Heck and I have a college degree. Actually, my real name is Hector, but everyone just calls me Heck. I got my degree at State U., home of the Fighting Bulldogs. Football is real big at State U. Well, to be honest, the "Dogs" weren't fighting "real good" when I was a student. In fact, they're still not fighting good, but that's because of the coach.

I went to State U. because somebody (I forgot who) told me it was real easy. Hey! Don't believe them! State U. is tough. Well it's tough if you don't know all the tricks about how to do good. As a student, I worked real hard to learn a bunch of tricks. Then everything got real easy. That's why it took me seven years to graduate. I had to learn all sorts of tricks.

When I graduated, I got this great job with Amalgamated Importers, just across town from State U. Then I went to Aruba for a couple of weeks where I got a huge, red letter D tattooed to my chest. When I got back, I made friends with Cliff who has a red letter O on his chest. Along with six other guys, me and Cliff spell out "Bulldogs" at all the State U. games. I made lots of money real quick at Amalgamated and then my friend, Cliff, got me appointed to the State U. Governing Board. A couple of years ago, I got on the Board on account of I got rich in my new job and because I go to all the Bulldogs games with a tattoo on my chest. Pretty neat, huh!

Now that I know lots of stuff about college, being a State U. Board member and all, I decided to write this book. It's about how easy it is to do real good in college—but you gotta know all the tricks, like speling and stuff. This book talks about classes and studying and football and there's even stuff about professors and deans and things. College is real serious, but I tried to make the book kinda funny.

Cliff is a real smart guy, so I let him read parts of my book before I sent it out to get published. Cliff made lots of changes, like he kept putting in complicated words nobody understands. Sometimes he changed whole pages and told me I have to use what he wrote. He says it's much better now, but I'm not so sure. When the book gets fancy and flowery, that's Cliff's doings. When it's real easy to understand, you'll know I wrote those sections by myself.

So, if you want to go to college, just read my book. It's full of wisdom. It will tell you all the easy tricks I learned about doing good at State U. The tricks are great! They'll probably work just about anywhere. Half fun!

Heck, State U. Board Member

SECTION I

PRE-COLLEGE KNOWLEDGE

Chapter 1

Hector's Hints on Picking a Real Good College

Colors for Your Den

The biggest decision you're likely to make in your whole life, second only to deciding what to wear or who to take to the high school senior prom, is what college to attend. Your choice will influence everything else in your life, like the color scheme of your den. This is real important. If you're a guy, like me, your den should be an expression of your favorite colors and your deepest values. You'll want your den to be a special place to relive all those great college memories, like the time you woke up everyone in the dorm quadrangle at 3:00 a.m. during finals week with firecrackers on long fuses planted in trees outside their windows. Your den is just the place for such recollections. You'll want to display in your den all your fraternity memorabilia like the cool beer mug you got at your frat initiation ceremony and the trophy your fraternity won for finishing first in intramural water basketball competition. Then there are all the college football souvenirs to show off in your den.

My den is great! On the wall over my bar, I've got an eighteen-foot-wide pennant with the State U. logo. All around the room are a zillion "Bulldogs" beer mugs and a bunch of other things with the school colors. State U. has great colors; red and gold. So everything in my den is red and gold. I've got a red wet bar--thirty feet long with real fourteen-carat gold trim around the edges. The bathroom tile and counter tops are red with gold flakes to match the gold sink and gold toilet. I don't dare tell my wife what I paid for my den. She'd kill me. My friend Cliff says I've got the best bar in town. He should know. He's tried them all. On the wall right behind the bar, I've got a giant copy of the letter appointing me to the State U. Governing Board. Cliff (he's been on the State U. Governing Board for years and years) got me appointed to the Board (see Chapter 19). Then he got Kinko's to blow up the appointment letter as big as a pool table. I framed the letter in red and gold and put it up over the bar. I am so proud of that letter and so pleased with my den! Cliff brings all the other State U. trustees and Board members over to my house to enjoy my den. It's just like being back in the frat again. Red and gold colors kick butt.

But what if your college's colors are black and blue? How would you ever explain this to your water-cooler buddies or bowling pals? Hey! Those are the colors of bruises. Black and blue means your team is a bunch of wimps who keep getting beat up. No thanks! Can you see yourself ten years from now swilling beer in your den with your old frat brothers and chanting the college fight song:

>Give me the Black
>Give me the Black
>Give me the Black, Black, Black
>Give me the Blue
>Give me the Blue
>Give me the Blue, Blue, Blue

Be honest! Would that song turn your crank a decade from now? Not a chance.

What if you went to a chi-chi, politically correct college with pink and lavender football colors? Could you feel proud in a pink and lavender den? Not me, buddy! You need to think about college colors before you make a mistake you'll always regret. You should prepare a list of your favorite colors as early as junior high school--say in seventh grade. Use the Internet to find out what colleges and universities have the best colors. If you're a guy, like me, you should consider only strong, aggressive, masculine colors like RED, GOLD, SILVER, and NAVY BLUE. These colors will make you justifiably proud of your college and your den. Whatever you do, don't pick a college with colors like SKY BLUE, MAUVE, or PEACH. Just ask yourself if you would want these colors haunting you all the rest of your life. No way!

College Mascots

Once you've settled on acceptable college colors, you should consider college mascots. They're so important. Mascots are more than fearsome animals, noble and powerful human figures, or unusual climatic conditions. They are more than lions and tigers and bears (Oh! My!). They are more than Trojans, knights, and midshipmen. The college mascot introduces your college and your football team to the entire outside world. You don't want a wimpy symbol.

Sometimes the name of the team is the only thing someone from another state knows about your college. Every person from Vermont, Ohio, or Mississippi, for example, will surely know that the major Florida teams are the Seminoles, Gators, and Hurricanes. But the out-of-stater is unlikely to know what city or what university these names represent. You might ask why the Ohio resident has even heard of these Florida teams. Simple! Each of these schools has a big-time football team that gets on ESPN a few times each year and even gets into bowl games. All Ohio residents care deeply about college sports. But Ohioans are more likely to know the won-and-loss record for the Gator football team over the past three seasons than the name of the city, Tallahassee, where the Florida State Seminoles (or is it the Hurricanes?) play football.

The Feminine Mascot

If you are a gal, preferring a more feminine-sounding mascot, you're in trouble. American colleges and universities began as masculine institutions (see Chapter 4), so their mascots are masculine as well. At best, a few college mascots are gender neutral, like "Cornhuskers." No mascots exist that might appeal, specifically, to young women. I never thought feminine mascots were a good idea. But we've got this gal, Phyllis, on the State U. Governing Board. She's a real feminist. When she heard I was writing this book, she made up a list of feminine mascot names and told me I have to put her list in the book. She's real tough. So I used her list. It's here in Table 1.1. You don't have to

Hey Doc! Does Speling Count?

look at the list, but at least it keeps Phyllis happy to have it in the book. You see, no American university or college has adopted one of these feminine names. I told Phyllis they wouldn't. They probably never will. So what's the point, Phyllis? The only feminine mascot in history was a climatic condition-- the "Hurricanes." This is because years ago all hurricanes were given female names like Hazel, Donna, and Camille. Those were great names for hurricanes. Thanks to political correctness, the National Weather Service now alternates names between masculine and feminine. So now we have to put up with dumb names like Bob.

TABLE 1.1:
HECTOR'S MASCULINE MASCOTS AND PHYLLIS' FEMININE ALTERNATIVES

FIGHTING IRISH	POTATO MASHERS
PANTHERS	PANTERS
GAMECOCKS	HEN PECKERS
SCARLET KNIGHTS	LADIES OF THE KNIGHT
TROJANS	DIAPHRAGMS
BULLDOGS	TOY POODLES
BOILERMAKERS	PETTICOAT MAKERS
HURRICANES	ZEPHYRS
MIDSHIPMEN	MIDWIVES
CRIMSON TIDE	BLUE LAGOON
BLUE DEVILS	WHITE ANGELS
TERRAPINS	BOBBY PINS
WILDCATS	PUSSYCATS
HUSKIES	PETITES
RAZORBACKS	SOWS
WOLVERINES	FOXY LADIES
NITTANY LIONS#	

As nobody seems to know what a nittany is, there is no feminine equivalent. Even Phyllis has no idea.

Scarlet Knights

As you think about college, be sure to select a mascot with real good name recognition. You want a strong, forceful, vibrant, masculine mascot like Scarlet Knights. Scarlet Knights has everything you could possibly want in a mascot name. It's got a great color (RED), a powerful male image with a fine suit of armor, and a firm anchor in medieval European mystique. Any college or university with such a fine mascot name has to be a winner. I know there's a Scarlet Knights university somewhere, but I can't seem to place it. Maybe it's in Wyoming or North Dakota or even Rhode Island.

Wherever it is, a university calling itself the Scarlet Knights would feature a spectacularly successful football program. It's probably had the same incredibly successful football coach for half a century. It must also have a brilliant and forward-looking president who knows how vital a winning college football team is. Probably the football team is the best in the country. Probably the Scarlet Knights' president is the most admired administrator who ever lived. You can just tell from the sound of the name, Scarlet Knights, that these things must be so.

I didn't know there were such great mascot names as Scarlet Knights when I was in high school. But when I started college, I picked a good one—the Gators. Too bad I flunked out. Just think how cool it would be if I were a Gator now. What a super football team! But it wasn't to be. So my dad helped me get into State U. The State U. Bulldogs are not a very good team, but the mascot is terrific. Bulldogs are almost as mean as Gators.

Duck

Don't pick something like Duck as a mascot. Duck is a weak, submissive symbol. The color of a duck is brown or, even worse, if it is a barnyard duck, white! Any self-respecting Scarlet Knight could blow a whole flock of Ducks right out of the air in ten seconds with a double-barreled crossbow. Duck is not good. If you get a degree from a Duck university, you're likely to wake up every night in a cold sweat from a recurring nightmare with people in duck suits quietly quacking behind your back.

Chicks

Many years ago, I learned what it's like having a bad mascot. At the tender age of twelve I suffered my first case of "bad-mascot trauma." I was selected in the Ft. Myers Babe Ruth League junior baseball draft to play for the Chicks. What an awful mascot! How I hated that name. Our team had canary yellow uniforms and canary yellow caps. We were the laughing stock of the league. But it could have been worse. If the coach had had his way, we would have worn orange tights under our baseball pants and displayed yellow pinfeathers across our backs. It was no picnic losing almost every game, but nobody on the team could hit or field.

The Chicks coach had wasted ninety percent of his draft points on a single prima donna kid (son of a Ft. Myers baseball legend) who didn't want to play baseball. He stunk at it as well. So, having almost no draft points left, the coach got nothing but the dregs of the draft. That included me. But I wanted to be real good at baseball, so I worked my butt off practicing. I ran up and down the beach every day to strengthen my legs and I threw millions of seashells way out into the water until I had the best arm on the team. I even practiced my swing in the living room until one day I smashed my mom's favorite table lamp. After I smashed a few more lamps, she forced me to practice baseball outdoors. By the time I started high school, I was pretty damn good at baseball (and lamp smashing).

Greenies and Gators

Our high school team mascot was a climatic condition--the Green Wave--another wimpy mascot if ever there was one. Our nickname was the Greenies. I played on the Ft. Myers High School baseball team under a coach who, after four seasons, still had not learned to spell the players' names. The lineup card always had "Heckter" leading off and playing shortstop. I kept telling the coach that my name is Hector, but he kept speling it "Heckter." He knew my nickname is Heck. I guess he figured my full name has "ter" tacked onto the end.

Just like the Chicks, we lost all the time. This time, it wasn't my fault. I did real good playing, but I never got over having my name misspeled. It was having that coach (who couldn't tell "Heckter" from "Hector") that made me decide to go to college. I wanted to learn how to spell people's names in case I ever had to write up a baseball roster myself. But there's not much speling in college any more. Not with computers and speling checkers. So don't worry about speling. You should focus on finding the best mascot instead.

It was not until I got to college that I finally had a real good mascot--the Gator. The Gator is a fine symbol of power, determination, and provoked aggression. We actually had a real, live, full-grown alligator mascot on the University of Florida campus. It lived in a huge wire cage right under the Florida bell tower. We all loved the Florida Gator and stopped by to visit with it every day during class change, with the bell tower blasting organ music overhead. Everything was fine until one night, after consuming about twenty-seven beers at a local 3.2 pub[1], the star running back for the U. of F. football

---

[1] Alachua County, Florida, was dry back then, so the bars and pubs could only serve beer that was 3.2 percent alcohol.

team broke into the cage and sliced through the Gator's tail with an ax. He was caught by a night watchman and suspended from the football team. This is all true. You can look it up. I liked the U. of F. but I busted out the first year. My grades were so low they wouldn't let me back in. But my dad knew this congressman guy so I got into State U.

State U. was just like U. of F., but it didn't have a real good football team. It was embarrassing going to State U. with such a losing football team. The team's been bad for decades, but me and Cliff are trying to fix things. On the Governing Board, we spend tons of money on State U. football. Next season could be the one.

Far, Far From Home

Almost as important as school colors and college mascot is the distance between your parents' home and the university campus. Pay particular attention to this distance. Too close, and your parents and relatives will drop in frequently. This is generally no problem. But some unannounced drop-ins could turn out to be embarrassing for all concerned--especially mortifying for that girl of the opposite sex you are just getting to know very, very well (Fig. 1.1). Oh, could I tell you about drop-ins. But that's another book.

College students never have enough money. "Broke" happens a lot in college, so you'll have to go home for money every chance you get. Be sure to take your dirty laundry home. It's too expensive to do laundry in college and it will make your mom feel special if you make her do all your college laundry. I saved up dirty laundry for days, just to please my mom. I even let her darn my socks and fix the zippers I broke yanking them open in moments of passion. She understood. The only time she complained was the time she found a 36D bra mixed in with my dirty laundry. I had a lot of explaining to do that day. But she bought the line about my getting my underwear mixed up with the fraternity housemother's stuff. She still believes this story. I've always been able to come up with real believable stories. So, bottom line, don't move too far away. If you are far from home, like the University of Hawaii or the Kamchatcka School of Socialism and Salmon Spearing, it will be hard to return on weekends when you're broke. Better stay closer to home. Figure on going home for money and laundry service about three times a month. Three hundred miles is a good distance.

(Fig. 1.1)

Chapter 2

Private vs. Public – So Many Choices

Do Not Disturb Sign

If you are ever going to get ahead in life, like I did, you need to pick a college or university with a real good reputation. Private, Ivy League colleges come to mind. Many private colleges and universities have real good reputations. They get their reputations on account of being real old and by having lots of rundown, granite-clad drafty buildings so covered in ivy you can't find the doors and you can't see through the windows (Fig. 2.1). Ivy League colleges charge extortionate[2] tuitions to make themselves appear exclusive. They have hordes of snooty professors who wear red polka-dot bow ties and brown herring-bone three-piece suits with black velvet elbow patches. The professors do nothing but smoke pipes while they write research grant proposals behind closed doors with "Do Not Disturb" signs

---

[2] My good friend Cliff—he's on the State U. Board too—he read this manuscript and changed a bunch of stuff. He put in this word. I don't even know what it means.

displayed at all times. A second sign shows the professor's office hour. This is the time he will see undergraduate students.

Office hour comes up once each semester--usually 8:45 to 9:45 a.m. on April 13 (unless that's Easter or Passover or National Bow Tie Appreciation Day). The office hour reappears in the fall from 4:15 to 5:15 p.m. on November 26 (unless that's Thanksgiving or the National Pipe Owner's Convention and Exposition or one of those strange holidays like Kwacha or Dreidel or Rhomboideus). If you wish to see the professor, plan to get in line at least a week in advance. You'll be glad you prepared for college by staying up all night on nineteen occasions trying to buy "Grateful Dead" concert tickets. While you're on line, the secretary across the hall will bring you coffee once in a while. She is used to seeing long lines in the hall on days before the professor's office hour. She thinks the professor you're waiting to see is a pain. I agree with her. Most professors at fancy, private, Ivy League colleges are snooty and stuck-up. But if you are nice to the secretary, she'll tell you some amazing stories about the professors. If nothing else, the stories help you to pass the time. Watch out, though. To spice up her life while her boss is locked behind that "Do Not Disturb" sign, she likes to hit on the seventeen-year-old guys. A week in line can be dull unless a well-preserved, middle-aged secretary pulls you out of line for a "quickie."

Since private colleges and universities lack big-time football programs, they can't get their reputations the usual way, by being on ESPN. It's tough for them. The ivy-covered, granite-clad buildings help a little. So do celebrity alumni who star in movies, host the Emmy Awards, or give anti-war, military disarmament talks at local tea parties and Rotary Club meetings. But these things don't help that much to build college reputations. So, in desperation, some private colleges try to rely upon the performance of their students and the reputations of their faculty. But who really cares about this stuff? Not me. Plus, faculty with reputations cost tons of money. That's why most private colleges have crummy football programs. All the money goes for prima donna professors, like that Einstein guy at Princeton. So to keep up appearances, private college professors sit around smoking pipes and writing research grant proposals behind closed doors. Private colleges are hung-up on research subjects like (1) how you can learn the age of a prehistoric painted turtle by the colors of paint the aboriginals put on its shell or (2) the proper way to dig up and catalogue microscopic pieces of Athenian pottery that smashed to bits when Mt. Vesuvius (or was it Mt. Etna?) erupted about 5000

(Fig 2.1)

years ago or (3) how to judge the climatic impact of that global warming crap or (4) what weird civilization came up with an instrument called the zither that nobody can play, let alone spell or pronounce. (Certainly nobody with a full set of teeth can pronounce zither.)

So private, Ivy League colleges think more grant proposals mean better college reputations. The same with tuition. The more you pay, the better the place seems. But if you go to a private, Ivy League college and your name is not Rockefeller or Vanderbilt or Gates or Trump, you really don't belong there and you will always feel out of place. I sure would of. That's why I went to State U. But, Hey! It's your call. If you like stuck-up colleges, go private.

But if you do go to a private college, you should change your name to Brook Shields, Britney Spears, Chelsea Clinton, or Bruce Springsteen. Changing names might help you fit in. But it won't solve your financial problems. To make tuition, you'll have to borrow tons of money or you'll need to sneak into a Brinks armored truck when the guard turns his head to watch a cute young thing cross the road. Unless you get lucky with that Brinks truck, you'll still be paying back student loans fifty years after graduation. If Social Security is still around, you'll need to use your retirement benefits to age eighty-three just to finish making tuition payments.

State U.

State universities are way bigger than small private colleges. Like State U., where I am, has more than 45,000 students. State universities don't cost near as much money and you won't have to wait in line for a week to see your professor. But you will crash into a language problem. While you'll be able to find your professor at a big state university, he or she will speak no English and will refer you to a teaching assistant who also speaks no English (see Chapter 3). Unless you were raised in Elbonia with Dilbert, you won't understand anything your professors are saying. Having to understand Elbonian accents is the down side to a big state university. Going to a university with a great reputation is the up side. The great reputation comes from big-time college sports. I wish they had big-time baseball in college. That's my sport. But, no. It's all football and basketball. So I'm learning to adjust.

The president of a large state university tries to make everyone living west of the Ural Mountains think his football team is the greatest in the world. The president talks about little else. His focus does change during second semester. Then he only talks about basketball. To get an idea how important college sports are, look at the salary paid to the head football coach. Real big bucks! The State U. head coach gets as much money as ninety-three college professors combined. I know. I did the math. But, hey! The coach is a whole lot more important than a bunch of liberal professors, even when he loses games like 83 to 6.

Everyone wants a football team with a longtime winning tradition, but winning requires a successful head coach. Successful head coaches don't come cheap. This is the way it should be. Your whole adult professional career (unless you take up catfish farming) will depend upon how successful your university football team has been over the past decade or two. Even if your football team sucks, no sweat, just as long as the team is considered big-time. If you graduate from a big-name football university, everyone will recognize your real good credentials. You'll get a great job real easy (about three days after you come back from your college graduation trip to Aruba-- finally sober). Hey! It worked for me. I got a super job right away with a local import/export firm, Amalgamated Importers, making all kinds of money (see Chapter 16). Then I got promoted in twenty-three days--all this because I went to a big state university with a big-time football program. Now, would you believe, I'm on the State U. Governing Board. Cool!

Chapter 3

Hector's Basic Training (You Gotta Start Early)

Hot Cars, Hot Chicks, and Hot Pop Tarts

As you near completion of ninth grade, your parents will start to nag you about college. They'll want you to start thinking about getting into a real good college. Mine bugged me every day for years. "Get good grades, Hector. We don't mean B's and C's, either. We mean A's. All A's! Understand? If you don't get A's, you're grounded, dammit."

I really got sick of all that nagging. I had other things on my mind like driving cars, dating hot chicks, and playing baseball every day. So I just took easy courses in high school—all the ones with general in front—like General Math, General Science, General History, General Wood Shop, General Bookkeeping, and General Eisenhower. And it worked. I got a bunch of A's. Best of all, I got to use Dad's car any time I wanted.

Dad's car had a brand new muffler, so the day I got my license I punched a bunch of holes in the muffler with a heavy-duty screwdriver so the muffler would sound real loud. That loud muffler moved me right to the top of the high school social ladder. You know, with four varsity baseball letters on my jacket and the loudest muffler in school, I was flying high.

What you take in high school is not too important. College admissions officers just want A's. To them, the grade of A in Beginning Pop Tarts is just as valuable as an A in Calculus. It makes admissions officers look good if the incoming students had all A's in high school. Admissions officers get merit pay increases based on the grade point average of each entering class. Hey! I'm on the State U. Governing Board. I vote on those pay raises. So listen up. If you make A's in General Math, General Wood Shop, and Beginning Pop Tarts, you'll do just fine. That's what I did and look where I am now. On top of the world.

Launching Fire Balloons and Writing Whole Sentences

College is very stressful. Once you get in, you'll start experiencing unusual demands--most of them social. You'll have more social activities than you ever imagined in high school. There will be football games, basketball games, rock concerts, dates, parties, intramurals, fraternities, sororities, and seventy-two hours-worth of non-stop homecoming events with open bar. Boy, did I have a blast at homecoming! I didn't miss a thing. Well, that's not exactly true. From halftime on, everything's just a big blur. You know, I carried into each game a set of fake binoculars that were really hollow flasks for booze. I filled them to both brims with 180-proof rum. I'm surprised the binoculars didn't dissolve. One of my frat brothers from Nassau always got high-test rum for me when he went back home. So, with all that rum I never really saw the second half of a football game—not once in seven years. I learned the scores from the newspapers when I woke up Sunday evening.

But not everything in college is social. You may have some academic demands too. Here my memory is a bit fuzzy. I remember studying a couple of times in college so I could stay eligible for fraternity softball. But that was about it. With the frat and stuff, I had no time left over for studying. Even back then, when college was cheap, I had to work forty hours a week in a fast food joint to make ends meet. Then I had all those college football and basketball games. No way was I going to miss any games (even if I had trouble focusing in the second half). When I wasn't working or going to games, I was doing real important fraternity stuff, like building homecoming

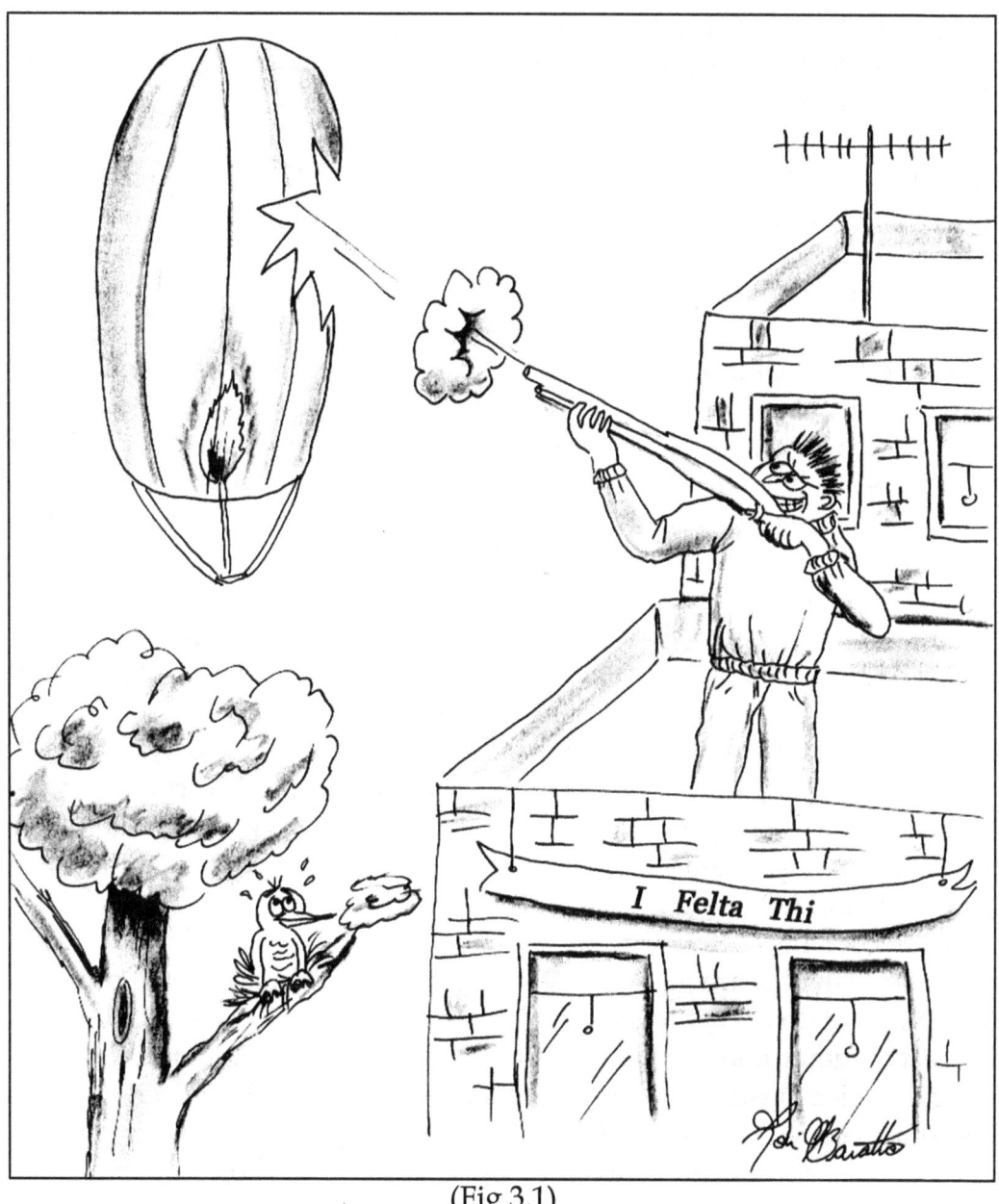
(Fig 3.1)

floats or playing intramural water basketball.

    I did so bad in my first semester at the U. of F. that, by Thanksgiving, I was mathematically eliminated from passing most of my courses. No sense studying for those finals. So, while everyone else in the frat was cramming for finals, I made a bunch of fire balloons from flimsy garment bags I got from the dry cleaners across from the frat house. The balloons worked real good.

Hey Doc! Does Speling Count?

My best one was as big as a phone booth. It carried a whole pint of flaming rubbing alcohol in a huge cotton wick. Take-off was picture perfect—just like a space shuttle launch. Then, as the balloon cleared the tree line in Gainesville, one of my frat brothers climbed out onto the roof of the house and blew my balloon out of the air with his shotgun (Fig. 3.1). It landed on a tree branch and quietly burned itself out. Lucky the whole town didn't catch on fire. If it had, they might have thrown me out of college even sooner. This is all true. You can look it up. So I guess you can see how much there is to do in college.

Well, back to class work. In some classes, you may be required to write complete sentences--all on your own. This is no joke. Some professors want real sentences--like, you know, ones with subject, predicament, and direct object. This is a bit extreme. But it happens. If you think you'll have problems writing whole sentences, make appointments to see your professors. Do this on the first day of classes (or at least before the drop date—the drop date is the last day you can drop a course without getting an F). Ask your professors if you have to answer test questions with complete sentences. A good approach (see Chapter 7) is to blurt out in a huge lecture hall, while the professor is deep in thought and oblivious ("oblivious" is another Cliff word) to the fact that the 632 seats (and all the aisles and fire exits) are full of students, something like, "Hey, Doc! Do you want whole sentences and stuff like that?" After some delay, as the professor regains his or her composure and the chuckling subsides, the answer will probably be, "No! All of your exams in NASDAQ Stock Tips will be multiple-choice."

That's good news. Stick with NASDAQ.

Whole sentences are just the beginning of the nightmare. Some professors will make you do essays. Watch out for essays. You don't want to do essays. In case you don't know what an essay is, here is a simple definition. While multiple-choice questions force you to use the letters A, B, C, D, and E, essay questions make you to use the whole alphabet. That's right. Essays go from A to Z. But you don't need essay courses. I wrote this whole book without a single essay course in college. I think it's real good. Don't you agree? So, if your professor says there will be some essay questions, you should drop the course on the spot. You don't need the hassle of essay courses.

If any of your college professors insists you write whole sentences and stuff like that, and you find this out after the drop date, your next choice should be to transfer to a real easy university. You'll probably want to transfer on the very next day. But transferring colleges at a moment's notice is not always prurient. (Or is that "prudent?" I'm not real sure). For example, despite some whole-sentence courses, your college might just happen to have the best football team in the entire hemisphere. Being in a college like this changes everything. Don't you dare leave! Leaving a college steeped in fabulous football tradition would be a dumb move. It ranks right up there with faking orgasms, changing religions, switching sexual orientation, or giving up eating collard greens and okra for the rest of your life. Don't treat this decision lightly. You may first want to consult with a priest or a psychic reader (they have very similar skills). Perhaps you want to do Freudian psychoanalysis for a year or two. But, no matter how you approach this decision, you are bound to conclude that leaving an upper-tier football university is too big a sacrifice for any student to make—essay questions or not. You better stay put. Like it or not, get used to the idea of stringing words together to create whole sentences.

Stringing words together is real hard work. There are literally hundreds of ways to put words together and many rigid rules about speling, grammar, style, and punctuation. You'll need to follow them all. So, if you are ever to get real good grades in whole-sentence courses, learn the rules!

Hector's Hints for Doing English Good

Some rules are easy. Take the TOPIC SENTENCE RULE. It says never to place more than six completely unrelated topic sentences in a row at the beginning of a paragraph. Six in a row is the limit. What's really best is to space your six unrelated topic sentences evenly throughout the first paragraph. Then, after about ten pages, you should say something about the topics you picked.

Another rule is called the PLURAL NOUN RULE. In case you've forgotten, nouns are words identifying persons, places, things, and unusual climatic conditions. Nouns are among the oldest parts of speech in the English language. When they first evolved, thousands of years ago, all noun was singular. Over time, a need for plural nouns emerged. Latin-speaking ancient Romans found a convenient way to create plural nouns by adding the letter "s" to the end of a word. This trick was then passed down from Latin to English. So, by the mere addition of an "s", singular words like "specie" can be converted into the plural form, "species." Such transitions have happened to hundreds of nouns. But, if you have not taken four years of Latin in high school, plural nouns may seem awkward. Table 3.1 could help. This table lists representative nouns and their corresponding plural forms. You may want to make a copy of Table 3.1 and carry it around in your wallet next to the ID card you altered so you can buy your own beer in campus pubs and watering holes. This way, you always get the speling right.

TABLE 3.1:
SPELINGS OF SOME INTERESTING NOUNS AND THEIR PLURAL COUNTERPARTS

one data	two or more datas
one alumni	two or more alumnis
one Homo sapien	two or more Homo sapiens (or Homos sapien)
one Rana pipien	two or more Rana pipiens (or Ranas pipien)*
one specie	two or more species
one criteria	two or more criterias
one phenomena	two or more phenomenas
one spectra	two or more spectras
one G. Bush	two or more G. Bushs (or G's Bush)

*In case you are not into biology, Rana pipien is Latin for frog. Because the names Homo sapien and Rana pipien rhyme, Charles Darwin figured that humans evolved from frogs. Some humans haven't changed that much over time. They're now called administrators.

If a sentence you write happens to contain both a noun and a verb, these parts of speech must agree with each other. This exciting rule is called the NOUN-VERB AGREEMENT RULE. It states that the verb must agree with the noun closest to it. The best way to learn this rule is by example. So study the following sentence carefully:

> Each of the datas were plotted on a graphs so every one of the phenomenas are clearly displayed.

In this example, the plural verb "were" agrees with the plural noun "datas," and the plural noun "are" agrees with the plural noun "phenomenas." In both cases, the verb agrees with the noun closest to it. Not a hard rule to follow.

The PERSONAL PRONOUN RULE (sometimes called the "never use 'me' when 'I' will do rule") states that the personal pronoun "I" should always follow a preposition. Never use "me." Using "me" in a sentence is real uncool. A sentence properly illustrating the personal pronoun rule follows.

All of the studying for this test was shared equally by you and I.

O.K. Are you clear on this? Should me and you go ahead with more rules of grammar? Good deal. Next comes the PRONOUN ANTECEDENT RULE. This rule states that the antecedent of a pronoun is always the noun closest in position to the pronoun. Check out this example.

> I constructed one bar graph, one line graph, and about twenty-seven real detailed, multicolor Power Point tables and then I wrote a brief summary for this report. It was the most effective part.

So, the antecedent of "it" is, of course, "report," because "report" is the noun closest to "it."

One of my all-time favorite rules is the ANTI-PARALLEL CONSTRUCTION RULE. Conforming to the older, parallel construction rule is archaic and boring. Parallel construction went out of style in the late 1960's. Much more interesting is the newer form of construction known as anti-parallel sentence structure. The idea behind anti-parallel construction is to mix things up a little so your sentences remain interesting to the reader. You don't want to be completely confined by rigid standards of sentence structure, probably created by Alexander the Great or Noah or King Tut. Be modern! Be creative! Make your sentences come alive. The following illustrates the anti-parallel rule.

> I finished the homework assignment in no time flat because it was interesting, had a lot of relevance to what I like doing, the TV was off, shorter than the last assignment, my roommate was out on a weekend date, and I need a new toner cartridge for my laser printer or I won't be able to do another assignment.

Do you see how much more interesting this is than parallel construction? I thought you would.

Most important among the whole-sentence rules is the WHEN TO USE AXE RULE. This is simple. You use "axe" when you are posing a question, but never when making a declarative statement. Don't confuse this kind of axe with the one the football running back used on the alligator tail. That kind of ax has no "e" at the end, just like the alligator has no tail on its end (see

Chapter 1). Here's an illustration of the WHEN TO USE AXE RULE.

> Hey, Doc! Should I axe my TA this question or will you axe her for me? Oh! Yeah. I didn't even axe you the question. Sorry. It's about how many axes I have to put on the graph.

There are several word preference rules you should master. These include, among others, the BRING-TAKE RULE and the FEWER-LESS RULE. Both rules can be summarized easily. Always use "bring" instead of "take" and always use "less" instead of "fewer." "Take" and "fewer" are old-fashioned words. They should never be used in modern English language. One example illustrates both rules:

> When you finish shopping, bring your cart to the cashier and be sure to use the aisle marked "ten items or less."

As you now know all of the important rules, you're probably ready to write your own whole sentences. If you feel comfortable with these rules, forget what I said about the college transfer thing. You should stay put. That is, unless there's a nearby school with a better football team. Football is much more important than whole sentences. So, if you're in a college with a nothing football program and you have a chance to transfer to a big-name football school (even one that requires whole sentences), do it. I know I said to keep away from whole sentences, but everything changes if you can transfer to a big-name football school. If so, pick a college that has the nation's best football team. I suggest one with "knights" and "scarlet" somewhere in the mascot name. You can't possibly go wrong when your college has such a real good mascot name. Well, not exactly.

If you want to launch fire balloons, you'll need to find a college with lots of wide-open space on campus. Urban colleges are not your best choice—fire hazard. Oh! What am I thinking? There's always the football field. Actually, football fields are great locations for fire balloon launchings, even in city colleges. There's lots of space and football fields are only used on Saturdays.

Hector's Hints on Misspeled Words

The English language has several troublesome words that are often badly misspeled. For these words, memorizing correct speling by rote is not an effective approach. As soon as you memorize the correct speling, you'll forget it and lapse back into some atrocious speling pattern. The only way to be sure that you are right is to copy the correct speling on the palm of your hand with a ballpoint pen. By the way, you should prepare for all college tests using this technique. Write all the answers on your hands. But, because college tests are real hard, you'll need more writing space than you did in high school. You will have to write answers on both palms. This requires an advanced degree of ambidextrose. If you can't write with each hand on the opposite palm, start practicing now. I couldn't be more serious. You absolutely have to work on this if you want to go to college. Still, you may need more writing space.

When I was a student, I let my arm get broken in flag football just so I could write answers on the cast. Breaking my arm hurt like hell, but it was worth the pain. That cast got me through a lot of tests. You'd be amazed how many answers you can squeeze on one arm cast. One time, when I had a real big test, a final exam I think, I laminated my cast and then peeled back layers of answers during the exam. I think I got 150 answers on that one cast.

By the way, some students now use fancy, electronic pocket computers to store all the answers to test questions. Don't do this. It's cheating. Students aren't supposed to lie or cheat—not until you graduate and become a lawyer or administrator. Then, all forms of deception are standard operating procedures. So, once you get the hang of writing clearly on both palms, check out Table 3.2. Table 3.2 shows a few troublesome words--the most commonly misspeled version first and the correctly speled version second. These are the first words you should be writing on your palms. Do it today! But don't use an expensive pen. The expensive ones have ink that never comes off. I can still read "excetera" clearly on my left hand. It's been there for years and years. It's sort of embarrassing, like an unwanted tattoo, but at least I always get the speling right.

Hey Doc! Does Speling Count?

TABLE 3.2:
HECTOR'S HINTS ON THE SPELING OF TROUBLESOME WORDS

SPELED INCORRECTLY	SPELED CORRECTLY
sepirate	seperate
iregardless	irregardless
ridicolus	ridicolous
libery	libary
ax a question	axe a question
exsetera	excetera
peninshula	peninschula
ekstablish	extablish
perifeal	peripheal
ekspecially	expecially
nucular	neucular*

*Listen careful to the speeches President Bush gives on foreign affairs. His pronunciation of neucular is perfect. He's got that word nailed. He's pretty good with irregardless and peninschula, too. He must have been coached a lot.

Hector's Hints for M/C Tests

Very few college classes require you to write whole sentences. They used to, but not much any more. It's too expensive to grade whole sentences. We're sure as hell not going to spend money to hire more faculty and teaching assistants to grade whole sentences at State U. (see Chapter 12). Not when we can't even get our football team to win a game. That would be nuts. So don't worry too much about whole-sentence classes. Certainly not at State U. Almost every test you take will have nothing but objective, multiple-choice (M/C) type questions (see Chapter 9 for a more complete discussion of the M/C test). This means, aside from writing your name at the top of the page, most of the writing you'll do in college is putting A's, B's, C's, D's, and E's on answer sheets. But the order of the letters matters a lot, just like the letters D, N, and A in DNA. Genes don't work if the letters are in the wrong sequence—like, maybe NDA. If your genes have the sequence NDA instead of DNA, you'll probably grow up to be a cucumber or something just as wierd. Likewise, M/C tests are no good if you get the order wrong. So don't be too complacent. Get the order right.

Some students have no idea what order to put down, so they copy someone else's M/C letters. There's lots of cheating in college. Be sure to cover your test paper carefully. You don't want anyone near you to get exactly the same grade—that is unless you're getting everything wrong. When you get everything wrong, you'll want your classmates to get zeroes, too. If you are getting everything wrong, act confident, as if you know precisely what you're doing. Write your answers real big. Let everybody around you see your real big answers. This way they'll copy your mistakes. The more people who copy you and get everything wrong, the better you place on the grading curve (see Chapters 10 and 11). That's pretty much what got me through college. Boy, did I ever lower the curve.

Practicing M/C Letters

To get ready for college, you should practice writing over and over again the first five letters of the alphabet--the ones that always come up in college-level multiple-choice questions. Don't try to do this practicing all at once. You should spread it out over time. I recommend starting early and working on one letter each year of high school. But there's a huge dilemma. If you finish high school in the usual four-year period of time, you'll have to double up on your letters one year. You'll need to practice five letters in just four years. Senior year is not the best time to schedule extra work. You will have all those college applications to fill out and you're bound to catch "senioritis" and you will be going to dozens of year-end parties. I recommend the practice schedule shown in Table 3.3

TABLE 3.3:
HECTOR'S PRACTICE SCHEDULE FOR GETTING REAL GOOD AT MULTIPLE-CHOICE QUESTIONS IN COLLEGE

High school freshman year:	Practice writing A's and B's 100 times each day
High school sophomore year:	Practice writing C's 100 times each day
High school junior year:	Practice writing D's 100 times each day
High school senior year:	Practice writing E's 100 times each day

You should take this assignment real serious and you should write your letter at least 100 times each day, including weekends. Spreading the burden out over four years will keep you from burning out before you start college. This way you can get off to a real good start. I didn't know about this practice schedule for like the first six years of college. Then it was almost too late. I really had to struggle.

If you're already a high school senior and you've never seen "Hector's Practice Schedule," I don't know what to say. I really don't. It may be too late for you. That's such a shame. I mean, what a shame if you never got through college just because you didn't know to practice your M/C letters in high school. There's no way you can do all the practicing in your senior year—no time. You can't write five different letters 100 times a day. Nobody has that kind of stamina. But, if you're determined, here's an idea. Why not enlist in the military for a few years? In the military, you'd have loads of time to work on your letters. They can't keep you that busy in the military. You know, there are only so many black boots to buff and so many smelly latrines to clean.

Hector's Hints on Numbers

High school guidance counselors usually advise college-bound students to bulk up on math. A counselor might suggest Algebra I, Plane Geometry, Algebra II, Solid Geometry, Trigonometry, and Pre-College Math. Your advisor might even tell you to take advanced math, perhaps Calculus, in your high school senior year. Pay no attention to this advice. You won't need much math to get accepted to college. In fact, you won't need any math at all. Pick yourself up from the floor. This is for real. I know this stuff. I'm on the State U. Governing Board, don't forget. You don't need math. Just take a bunch of general wood shop and beginning Pop Tarts courses and make sure to get all A's. Colleges are used to students who are hopeless in math. So they've made curricular adjustments. College math departments have created lots of remedial math courses. I think there were only two remedial math courses when I was a student, but they keep adding new ones. Now State U. has zillions. They exist to correct math deficiencies as far back as first grade.

The entry-level math course for science majors in college used to be Calculus I. I never took Calculus. I thought Calculus I was an old Roman emperor or something, but it's really a math course. Very few of today's students are ready for Calculus I or any other college math class. So, unless you're one of those math geeks, just skip high school math and wait until college where you have your choice of exciting remedial math courses. There's a rich selection. Table 3.4 lists the remedial math courses currently offered by State U.

TABLE 3.4:
REMEDIAL COLLEGE MATH COURSES OFFERED AT STATE U.

Mathematics 227	Pre-Calculus I
Mathematics 206	Pre-Claudius I
Mathematics 205	Prep for Pre-Claudius I
Mathematics 9 ¾	Imaginary numbers (two semesters)
Mathematics 10E9 BC	Carboniferous-Era Math (Use of Graphitic Implements in Arithmetic Calculations)
Mathematics XLIV	Pre-Historic Math (two millennia)
Parabolic Functions 36-24-35	Harmonically Coupled Oscillators in Non-Linear Algebras
Emerging Wave Functions 25-22-25	Pre-Algebras with Dampened Oscillators
Planar Theory 20-20-20	Pre-Teen Linear Algebras
Mathematics XXX	String Theory and G-String Theory
Mathematics X (1/X)	Achieving Cosmic Singularity by Multiplying Reciprocals (Theory and Practice)
Mathematics 052	Arithmetic (Taught by the Tune of a Hickory Stick)
Mathematics 015	The New York Times Tables
Mathematics 1-9	Basic Counting
Mathematics 009	Introduction to the Nine Non-Zero Duck Pins
Mathematics 01234	Readiness Skills for Learning Your Numerals (First Semester)
Mathematics 56789	Readiness Skills for Learning Your Numerals (Second Semester)

    The first thirteen courses are real tough, so most students begin with Math 1-9 and then work up the list. Some students drop Math 1-9 when they discover that Math 1-9 is not Basic Accounting. Although the names sound alike (Basic Counting and Basic Accounting), these courses are real different. Math 1-9 is much harder. Believe me! I sat in on Math 1-9 for a couple of classes. Real challenging! Board members and trustees observe classes once in a while when we think the professors are being too tough. Then we write letters to the professors to get them back in line. Cliff calls it lowering the bar. I'm not sure what he means by this.

    So, if you're weak in mathematics, remember this advice. Don't panic. There's always a place for you in a college remedial math class. Us guys in the State U. administration want to keep you in college. So it's O.K. to take all seventeen remedial math courses. More courses mean more money for the administration. If you need to stay an extra year or two or seventeen to take remedial courses, no sweat. That's why we have remedial courses. They keep you in college. You just have to be sure your parents pay your $24,920 in-state tuition each year plus all those add-on fees. By the way, you'll have add-ons for housing, student activities, parking, student newspaper, computer systems for the administration (see Chapter 21), interest on twelve state bond initiatives for silly research centers, and UPCA.

The President's "Kiwi" Supplement Proposal

Oh! I haven't explained UPCA. Pay attention! UPCA is the University President's Clothing Allowance. His $525,000 annual salary doesn't cover his clothing. So, at a special Board meeting we voted in UPCA. Cliff and I voted against UPCA because we don't like the president. But we lost the vote. The others voted yes, just so the president wouldn't show up at Board meetings in his birthday suit. That would be disgusting. But I wouldn't put it past him. He is so used to university handouts he resists spending his own salary money for anything personal. He'd rather show up naked than to spend a single penny of his salary on personal clothing—State U. pays for his clothing.

By the way, the president gets a whole lot more than $525,000 when you add in all his perks, incentives to stay for at least five years (an additional $500,000), and special gifts. He's loaded. In addition to UPCA, he gets free catered food, free entertainment, free housing, free legal services, free IRS advice, free postage, and free maid and butler service. He also gets a free personal chauffeur, free travel, free gardeners, free health insurance, free psychic readings, free acupuncture treatments, and free whole-body massages. He even gets free Gideon Bibles placed in the nightstands of each of his twenty-seven bedrooms and free door-to-door delivery of Watch Tower Magazine. He has free retirement, free college tuition for up to forty relatives, and as many free NFL and NBA tickets as he can possibly use (see Chapter 17).

So, how does he spend all his salary money? We're not sure. Maybe he squirrels every cent away in a Swiss bank account. Well, that's not exactly true. He has to pay for the black shoe polish he smears all over his hair. Shoe polish came real close to becoming a free perk of the State U. presidency. By a slim majority, the Board voted down his "Kiwi Supplement Proposal." He took that defeat real hard. But now we know he has at least one expense—

black shoe polish. Everything else is paid by the state.

But, unlike the president, you'll have a variety of expenses. Lots and lots of expenses. One of them is parking fines. Don't forget to budget for parking fines. There are ten times as many students as there are parking spaces on the State U. campus, so expect to collect about 712 parking tickets (at $35 a pop) every year. You'll note that this amount ($24,920) exactly matches the annual tuition. They plan it that way so the university accountants can estimate income by multiplying your tuition by two. I'm still paying off parking fines and I've been out of college for years. The administration will also encourage you to attend all the football and basketball games where you'll blow hundreds of dollars just for binoculars (see Chapter 20). Don't worry about parking for the football games. All around the stadium, there's convenient parking for 138,900 football fans and they never give out tickets to the fans. So you won't get ticketed unless you park directly on the 50-yard line.

What Ranglege You Speak?

It may surprise you that all major universities in the United States are multilingual. This blew me away, but it's true. There's all sorts of foreign languages. But not everything in college is foreign. There is some English too. Like, university catalogs are printed in English and the pre-admission orientation for prospective students and their parents is conducted in English. All of your multiple-choice tests will be written in English as well. However, sixty-three percent of your classes will be delivered in Chinese, Japanese, or Korean by professors or teaching assistants who arrived on campus two weeks before you did. State U. can't afford expensive American professors, so we get discount professors from anywhere we can find them. They're a lot cheaper if we import them by the boatload (Fig 3.2). The discount professors all get a one-week-long crash course in conversational English by the Dean of Instruction. So, "no plobrem." Right away the discount professors are able to go into huge lecture halls to face 632 students. Despite their lack of communication skills, they all know how to give multiple-choice tests and then how to curve your grade (see Chapters 10 and 11).

The other thirty-seven percent of your classes will be presented in various erotic foreign languages, including Hindi or Urdu (13%), Farsi (6%), Arabic (5%), Armenian (4%), Latvian (2%), English (2%), and other (5%). You'll get used to this. Everybody does. A useful way to prepare for the multilingual college is to learn some common expressions in a variety of erotic foreign languages. Near the back of most college catalogs you will find lists of useful

Hey Doc! Does Speling Count?

English expressions translated into foreign languages. Table 3.5 is such a list from the catalog of a large West-Coast university. State U. has a table like this too. Memorize Table 3.5 before you even think of attending an American university. I'm serious. This is real important. I wish I'd thought to do this myself. But I was too back woods then.

(Fig.3.2)

TABLE 3.5:
COMMON ENGLISH EXPRESSIONS TRANSLATED INTO AN EROTIC EASTERN LANGUAGE

That's not right	Sum Ting Wong
Are you harboring a fugitive?	Hu Yu Hai Ding?
See me ASAP	Kum Hia Nao
Stupid man	Dum Gai
Small horse	Tai Ni Po Ni
Did you go to the beach?	Wai Yu So Tan?
I bumped into a coffee table	Ai Bang Mai Ni
I think you need a face lift	Chin Tu Fat
It's dark in here	Wai So Dim?
I thought you were on a diet	Mun Ching?
This is a tow away zone	No Pah King
You are not bright	Yu So Dum
I got this for free	Ai No Pei
Please stay a while longer	Wai Go Nao?
Stay out of sight	Lei Lo
He's cleaning his automobile	Wa Shing Ka
Your body odor is offensive	Yu Stin Ki Pu

Ten Pelcent Passing in Amelican Correge

Don't be concerned if you understand nothing your college instructors say. This is perfectly normal. I couldn't understand most of my professors and teaching assistants when I went to State U. That was even before State U. started hiring discount professors, the ones who never learn English. Language is no big deal. Even if you get a professor who speaks fluent English, you won't understand anything in subjects such as Physical Chemistry, Indiscreet Algebras, Computer Sciences, and Statistics. Nobody ever understands these subjects, so you won't be alone. No teacher in the history of college education has been able to explain anything in these four subjects. So they're always taught by persons speaking no discernable English. Textbooks for these courses are written to impress the one person in the world more knowledgeable than the author. Even the author has no clue what the book means. With an unintelligible textbook and a non-English speaking teacher, the class average is seldom more than ten percent. If you luck out and get twelve percent as your final average in Physical Chemistry, for example, you will probably place near the top of the curve and you will get at least a B+ in the course.

If you are hoping to do better than a B+ in college courses, you should probably take four years of Chinese in high school and work in an authentic Chinese take-out restaurant sixty hours a week each summer to maintain your language skills. At least this way you will remember that R is L and L is R. This a learry impoltant skirl to realn for Amelican correge.

Section II

So You've Chosen State U., My Alma Mater

Chapter 4

Hector's History of State U.

Get Aquainted

Most colleges and universities try to make freshmen feel comfortable in their transitions from high school. As a way to help you get acquainted, they present short histories of higher education in their catalogs and web sites. State U. is no exception. Beginning on page 663 of the State U. catalog is a chapter called the "Get-Acquainted" section. The president thinks the State U. "Get-Acquainted" section is great. He wrote it; that's why. I think it's dumb and boring. Plus, nothing is right. So I've written my own "Get-Acquainted" section that tells the truth about college in real common English. I did loads of research so I would get everything just right. My "Get-Acquainted" section is here in Chapter 4. My writing is real well done and it's much more fun than the president's stuff. I wrote everything myself, even though Cliff didn't like some of it. Too bad, Cliff. It's my book.

These days, just about everybody goes to college. I bet you will too. We hope you will choose State U.; but before you consider attending any college, you should learn a bit of the history of higher education in America. It's important for you to know something about college life as it was in the Dark Ages--your parents' generation and the generations before. A quick look at State U. history will tell you many interesting things about Mom and Pop and your grandparents, aunts, and uncles. These folks did some wild and crazy things in their college years. You'll be amazed. So, gather the whole family together as you take a little journey back into the past. You'll have fun reading "Hector's History of State U." and so will they. As my story unfolds, I'm sure you'll recognize several of your favorite relatives.

Stata U.

State U. has a rich and proud heritage. It was founded in 1492 by a small band of Italian immigrants who sailed to America in three tiny wooden boats, the Nina, the Pinta, and the Loco Parentis. Drinking cheap Italian wine, full of sulfites and other carcinogens, and singing "Oh Mine PaPa" throughout the cruise, these brave mariners crashed into a famous East-Coast rock and promptly founded the first colonial university. They named their new university Stata U. Knowing only one religion, these Italian mariners established Stata U. as an all-Catholic, right-to-life, rhythm-method university. The Stata U. name lasted about three days, as a bunch of militant Quakers quickly overthrew the Stata U. Catholics and sent them all back to Italy in their three tiny wooden boats. The Quakers put down their oatmeal and immediately renamed Stata U. They called it State U., a name that has persisted for more than five centuries.

State U., like other universities in the American colonies, was patterned after the great universities of northern Europe—elite boarding schools for sons of the aristocracy. In boarding schools like State U., wealthy landowners sequestered their sons from the real world and all its problems. We still train our future American presidents and many congressional leaders in such institutions. No wonder some politicians cannot relate to the needs of the general public. They've never been part of the general public. But that's another subject. The primary function of the early American university was to serve as a training ground for boys entering the Protestant clergy. The fledgling country, founded on the basis of religious freedom for all, tolerated just one faith--Protestantism. If early colonists did not attend Protestant services every Sunday, they had to spend the rest of the week with their hands and heads stuck in a big piece of heavy wood called the stock exchange. All day long, passers-by taunted the people stuck in the stock exchange with nasty remarks like, "Well, Benjamin, how much money have ye lost in the stock exchange today? Perhaps you'd do better in bonds."

For centuries, State U. flourished as a male-only religious training school for boys whose parents sent them to college to become monks, elders, bishops, vicars, deacons, ministers, divine creationists, holy rollers, tea-totalers, serpent handlers, fire walkers, door-to-door proselytizers, Watch Tower columnists, tin-can-phone evangelists, religious bigamists, circumcisionists, or other practitioners of the sacred arts. Colonial boys were sent off to college in their early teens. That's because their parents were too embarrassed to explain nocturnal emissions to them. The girls stayed back on the farms feeding chickens, milking cows, cavorting in the barn with farm hands, and learning from them (the farm hands, not the cows) the supine facts of life.

In Loco Parentis

Miles away from parents and community, State U. boys were carefully watched day and night by college administrators so as to keep them away from sex. Keeping boys away from sex was a big job for a college administrator in those early days. One thing that helped was the cold shower. Did you know that the cold shower was invented right here at State U? It's true. The patent was issued in 1503. The cold shower is one of State U.'s most famous inventions--second only to the cold shoulder. The cold shoulder came much later--right after State U. became co-ed. Some psychologists still recommend the cold shower for frisky young men. More enlightened professionals suggest football as a way for males to act out their sexual aggressions.

But early college administrators paid no attention to football. Football had not yet been invented. For several hundred years, administrators had nothing with which to work but cold showers and coerced sexual abstinence. Generally they chose coerced abstinence. As religiously grounded State U. administrators were uncomfortable with the slightest allusion to sex, their abstinence policy needed a subtle name—something catchy, mysterious, and convoluted. Their first choice was "Just Say No." But, as compelling as "Just Say No" can be, it was a bit too risqué. An expression in Latin would be perfect. But the only Latin phrase they had ever seen was the expression on the stern of that tiny Italian boat. So they went with it. Many years later, to their total chagrin, these sanctimonious scholars learned the literal translation of "in loco parentis" was "keep it in your pants." Despite this huge semantic setback, the name stuck and the "loco" doctrine became firmly established at

State U. and throughout the colonies.

State U. used to have a real big thing (no pun intended) about morals, so the "loco" doctrine hung around (I hope you don't think this is another pun) for nearly five centuries. The doctrine was still in place when I enrolled at State U. We even had a Lesser Associate Dean of Sexual Abstinence whose job it was to guide our moral development. I think his name was Dean Hail, but students called him Lesser Hail. A few days before classes began, Lesser Hail herded all the guys (more than two thousand of us) into one monster auditorium and talked to us man-to-man about clean living. His talk was real inspiring. He taught me a bunch of things I never dreamed people do. I kept going back to Lesser Hail's clean-living talks. He gave one every few weeks. I attended each one—front row, center. I wanted to be sure I understood how to do everything he talked about. Later, I tried a few things he warned us about. Then a few more. Then a whole lot more. Wow! They were pretty neat. They still are, but that's the subject for another book.

Utter or Udder

By the turn of the 19th century, the leaders of the American aristocracy were all college- educated men. Many were educated at good old State U. But these men were growing tired of always marrying milkmaids--especially milkmaids who weren't always innocent maids-a-milking, if you get my drift. They wanted wives who, in polite social conversation, would at least know the difference between utter and udder. Out of this need for sophisticated conversation grew the first colleges for women. Then, as the scholastic separate-sex movement declined through the 20th century, education embarked upon a major experiment. All-male colleges began accepting women. These first co-ed colleges were not like those we know today. They were segregated--hormonally segregated. Residential estrogen was restricted to the south side of campus, testosterone to the north.

Sex Hormone Intermingling

Sex in college first became possible in the mid-1900's, but never after 10:30 p.m. At exactly 10:30 p.m., in colleges all over the country, two-hundred-pound Amazons, called resident assistants, herded all the girls behind locked dormitory doors. Then, every night, at exactly 10:41 p.m., the Amazons conducted bed checks by pulling the fire alarm. Missing bed check was a very serious morals infraction. It was even worse than chewing gum in high school. An empty bed implicated the missing co-ed in an act of off-campus cohabitation. Such an infraction could lead to expulsion from college. The only rules infraction more serious than off-campus cohabitation was on-campus double occupancy in a single bed. Lesser Hail warned us about cohabitation, but I guess he never tried it. I did! Lots of times. It's loads of fun. I still get away with cohabitation once in a while. Don't tell my wife, O.K? She's not very understanding. But the early 1960's standards were about to undergo a radical change. The hippies were coming.

Here Come the Hippies

If you don't know about hippies, ask your parents or older relatives, watch some re-runs of "The Wonder Years" on TV, or check out the play "Hair" in your community theater. The hippies were an interesting bunch. I'll bet you'll discover lots of ex-hippies in your own family tree. They're the ones in family portraits with tie-dyed tee shirts, self-rolled cigarettes, and faces completely covered with hair. The boys, that is. We had at least one full-fledged hippie in our own family. I don't think it was tobacco he rolled in his cigarettes. No! It wasn't me. I was as straight as an arrow back then. I've only become wierd recently. (Damn! Is that "i" before "e" or the other way around?) The hippie generation of the 60's and 70's marked the death of "in loco parentis." It was the era of sexual revolution. The old taboos vanished as free love became the rage. I totally missed the era of free love--I was married by then.

The Atonal Jackhammer

Many campus traditions have vanished--like music that sounds good. I bet that your parents agree with me about this. So do your grandparents. Gone is the "king of rock and roll." Gone are the Beatles, BeeGees, and Everly Brothers. Gone, too, are gentle, beautiful, melodic ballads. Gone are The Brothers Four, the Kingston Trio, Simon and Garfunkel, and Peter, Paul, and Mary. Gone are the Carpenters, John Denver, Glen Campbell, and Pat Boone. Gone from the college scene are The Lettermen, the only trio in the history of music to have mastered nine-part harmony. They're all gone. There is new music on campus now. I don't pretend to understand the new music. Your parents and grandparents don't either. Alley cat sounds seem to be an important element. So is inserting at least eighty-three extra notes from non-harmonizing voices into each musical measure. There is also a desire to utilize every wall in the building as a massive basso soundboard. If you cannot see the walls violently resonating with scads of megawatt sub-woofers, it's not the new campus music. They've even put campus music on the Richter scale. It's an 8.1--almost as loud as a college basketball game or a football victory celebration at the Watering Hole on University Avenue.

State U. student apartments have sustained substantial sub-woofer damage. So last year the Governing Board decided to limit sound systems to no more than twelve sub-woofers per room. This decision came to be known as the State U. sub-woofer rule. The sub-woofer rule is the one thing we accomplished on the Board last year. As I recall, that's about all we did except to fire the football coach and raise the president's salary. I don't like sub-woofers, so I worked real hard on the sub-woofer rule. In fact, I go far out of my way to avoid deep bass sounds on campus. This is not easy. The sub-woofers seem to track down, corner, and then acoustically torture every person over the age of thirty. A new musical instrument called the atonal jackhammer is responsible for the torture. On an average day, an estimated 1.86 million atonal jackhammers broadcast their sounds from within 297,000 college apartments to every corner of the country. The sound is so pervasive it encircles the globe and reflects back off Jupiter on a clear night. Acoustic engineers have directly linked Jupiter's newly observed pockmarks to the relentless impact of college music. Some naïve amateur astronomer, who is just a shoemaker in real life, reported the Jovian pockmarks to be caused by the impacts of a fractured comet. This is udder nonsense.

Co-Ed Rooms and Kinky Clothes

In recent decades, everything on campus has changed. The Amazons are all gone. So there are no longer any bed checks. Ask your mom and grandma about this. They'll tell you that nobody misses the Amazons or the bed checks. Gone, too, are unisex dormitories, all replaced by co-ed apartments. The apartment doors are still locked at 10:30, but with several boys and several girls locked inside each bedroom. You can bet they are not sleeping. Damn! Co-ed bedrooms. I missed all this. Maybe I should go back to college and start over again.

Gone from the college scene are the miniskirts. They literally vanished when hemline finally met waistline. Think that over for a moment. Hemline met waistline. Got it? Your mom will remember the minis. Boy, do I ever! She probably has a bunch of old miniskirts in a cedar chest somewhere around the house. She'll be too embarrassed to admit it. When she is out playing bridge one night, check out the cedar chest. It's a good idea to keep a few miniskirts for yourself. They'll probably come back in style in a few years—

but this time it could be a guy thing to wear a miniskirt. People just get wierder and wierder. (I can never spell that word. It's that "i"—"e" rule again. Oh! Whatever!)

Throughout the 80's and 90's, trends in college fashion moved toward unisex clothing—clothing that revealed nothing personal except the names of the clothing manufacturers. Both genders started wearing two-hundred dollar untied designer tennis shoes and overpriced baggy sweats ornamented in bold letters with the manufacturer's logo. Great marketing scheme! Charge big bucks to allow the buyer to advertise your products. Not even Tom Sawyer thought of this scam. One manufacturer's logo offers the message "All Day I Dream About Sex." Dreaming about sex was about all that a State U. student could do in the 80's and 90's when nobody could identify another's gender. Hidden behind yards of baggy denims and XXXXL sweatshirts, all State U. students, male and female, began to look alike. By the mid-90's, unisexness reached crisis proportions. Not only were there unisex clothes, but there were unisex first names, unisex beauty parlors, unisex bathrooms, unisex jewelry, unisex tattoos, and unisex hair styles. State U. students became totally unable to distinguish one sex from the other (Fig. 4.1). Gametic exchange took an unprecedented nosedive. Folks, this was not a good time to invest in Pablum and Zwibacks.

Gender I and Gender II

Sponsored by leading baby food companies, a series of non-credit gender-identification classes sprang up on campus. The aim was to teach students how to spot members of the opposite sex, the assumption being that they would take things a step further. At State U., students packed the Gender I and Gender II courses. My niece, Stacy--or is Stacy my nephew, I'm not sure--took both Gender ID courses. She/he said they were real tough. The worst parts, Stacy said, were the morning sickness and ankle swelling. But these classes helped tens of thousands of confused students learn how to spot members of the opposite sex. Gender ID courses also revitalized countless moribund sociology and psychology departments. At State U. and elsewhere, departments searching for some form of post-60's identity filled the intellectual gap with courses in gender ID. Sociology and psychology departments are pleased with the gender ID outcome. So is Gerber.

(Fig. 4.1)

Drop the Waistline

By the end of the 1990's, fashion designers realized that unisexness (like Kansas City in Rogers and Hammerstein's "Oklahoma") had gone just about as far as it could go. They needed a new trend. Gender ID courses were not enough. Somehow, some way, clothing had to reveal some hint of a student's gender. The fashion industry's solution was elegant. Drop the waistline! This revolutionary fashion trend came, at the turn of the millennium, in two successive waves. First came the hip-hugger jeans. What a great idea!

Coupled with extra short tops, hip huggers offer just a hint of gender. They also show off the latest in bellybutton jewelry. Even with hip huggers, students remained somewhat unsure of the genders of others. A second fashion wave did the trick. It lowered the waistlines again to produce the incredibly provocative sub-hip hugger. With sub-hip-hugger jeans, gender is no longer in doubt.

Cleavage gazing has always been a popular campus sport. When I was younger, I would sneak a look at women's cleavages every chance I got. I still try now and then. But the only cleavages I see on campus these days are the hairy backsides of guys wearing their sloppy, droopy, sub-hip-hugger shorts supported only by their knobby knees. Not quite what the fashion industry had in mind.

Years ago, knee-length pedal-pushers and Bermuda shorts were the rage. Now they're out. Popeye-style bellbottoms are back in style--but with longer inseams. The most popular inseam length at State U. is ninety-seven yards. Long, baggy pants have some advantages-- especially if you have been drinking too much. With long pants, you can go to the bathroom at a State U. football game and your own cuffs will stay behind to save your seat. If you're stone drunk, you can retrace your pants legs right back to the block of seats where the rest of your fraternity brothers are located. Don't trip on your untied shoelaces. Hopefully the guys haven't killed the keg you so cleverly smuggled into the stadium. Now that's a college skill that really means something.

The Uvula Ring

The new millennium has changed the college scene forever. Gone from campus are long hair-styles that made students look like English sheep dogs jubilantly scrambling from ponds of axle grease. (Don't get axles confused with axes or axes — see Chapters 1 and 13.) Gone is body paint. Body paint was just too temporary. Especially in the rain. Body mutilation is now in style. It comes in three basic forms — tattoos, body piercing, and ear removal. Ear removal was introduced in the 19th century by a wacky guy named van Gogh. He reportedly mailed his ear to a girl friend. As legend has it, she was not impressed. So ear removal quickly went out of fashion. An attempt to resurrect the practice was made in the latter part of the 20th century by Mike Tyson, but it never really caught on the way Tyson thought it might. So we are left with tattoos and body piercing as the millennial ways to attract a mate. In this new adornment culture, each student competes to see how much

Hey Doc! Does Speling Count?

(Fig 4.2)

stainless steel his or her torso's tender tissues can support. The modern record, I've been told, is 127 pounds of heavy metal. While quite compelling, body piercing does have its problems. Homeland Security Cabinet Minister, Tom Ridge, prevents tin-plated passengers from setting foot on commercial airplanes. You'll trigger every metal detector in the airport, even before you reach the terminal. But some body piercing is tantalizingly attractive. My favorite is the uvula ring (Fig 4.2). Soooo----sexy.

Football Vs Catfish Farming

Colleges have always been the pacesetters in style and sexual practices. But the greatest educational gift to America, second only to co-ed bedrooms and uvula rings, was the development of intercollegiate football. College football evolved from the 19th century battle between Princeton and Rutgers. Rutgers won that famous 1869 match with Princeton six to four. Countless decades have passed and Rutgers is still trying to regain the glory of that fleeting moment. Perhaps next season. Since most major college and university administrations place football at the center of campus activity, you'll want to focus your socializing accordingly. You see, at State U., after we pay the football bills, there's just not much money left for other activities. Education is not very high on our list of university priorities. Plus, teaching is just too expensive, even with discount professors and such. So, if you don't like football, college may not be the place for you. Try State U. for a while and, if you don't like football, just drop out. Remember it's never too late to drop out of college. People do it every day.

So instead of blowing the next four years trapped in a football culture you might not like, think about catfish farming. Catfish farming is a good, honest trade and there's not much competition. But never tell your parents you sank their $96,427 tuition reserve into some fishy scheme. This has to be a secret. You'll need special training to pull off a tuition switcharoo. So it might be a good idea to take Economics 111 (Secretly Investing Your Parents' Tuition Check On Wall Street). Economics 111 explains everything. There's a whole chapter in the Eco-111 textbook on how to avoid getting caught by your parents. But, in case you confess or something stupid like that, there's another chapter that tells you how to deal with your parents' reactions to your ripping off their hard-earned money. If your parents ever find out you've blown their tuition money to buy a bunch of fish, they could be ticked off, especially if they don't like fresh water catfish. Would you blame them? Hopefully, you won't get yourself into this sort of mess. But, in case you do, be sure to register for Economics 111 early. The course is always jammed.

Carp Gulping and Granddad's Porn

The agricultural and industrial revolutions ushered in sweeping changes in college life. Your parents probably don't remember this, but they've surely heard about it. Suddenly, in the mid-1800's, there was need for a non-aristocratic, non-ecclesiastical (another of Cliff's notes), skilled workforce. The economy demanded college-educated men to run factories and farms and to manage growing teams of business workers. Parents now had reasons other than "in loco parentis" to get their kids out of the house. Colleges had begun to offer training in real job skills for students lacking pedigrees. Business, finance, management, astrology, phrenology, alchemy, lobotomy, fluoroscopy, leechless medicine, and what to do with urban horse dung all became new areas of academic action in colleges throughout the country. By the 1900's, college students expected more than an education in these emerging academic fields. They wanted some fun too. But the "loco" doctrine still put a zipper on the most appealing recreational option—at least for the boys. So students of the 1920's supplemented their studies with other recreational activities—like swallowing live goldfish. With this form of oral gratification, no wonder the stock market crashed. These ex-carp-gulpers had become the brokers of 1929.

By the 1950's, college kids had learned to stuff themselves, by the dozens, into phone booths and small cars. The body contact led to bigger things. Sex came out of the closet. Male students of the 1950's spent more time sweating over Playboy than reading boring college textbooks. That same generation of students perfected the venerable Cold War military tactic known as the panty raid. Lesser Hail warned us about panty raids, too. We listened very intently. These operations need to be done skillfully. It helped having an experienced administrator advising us on how it's done.

The girls were not sitting idly by either. They all tried to lure the boys into their off-limits dorms by looking like Marilyn Monroe with bleach-blond hair, padded bras, and flared skirts. The bikini burst (or should that be busted?) onto the scene along with the jitterbug and the hop. It was an exciting time to be young. But even the most daring panty raider could not have predicted what was to follow his generation. State U. students of the early 1970's brought the sexual revolution to a social climax. They invented mass streaking in the nude. This is no joke.

Streaking caught Lesser Hail completely by surprise. There was nothing in his clean-living talks about streaking. We had no administration help here. Everyone had to learn by personal experience. And learn we did. Overnight, students transformed the campus. The little patches of lawn surrounded by stately four-story buildings in sedate campus quadrangles became as provocative as that famous nude beach in San Diego. Naked bodies were everywhere, appearing mysteriously and rushing from corner to corner across the quadrangles. As soon as 100 streaking bodies vanished behind trees or around buildings, another 200 took their places. Suddenly, there was more sex on campus than in a lifetime's collection of National Geographic magazines. Your granddad will know all about campus streaking. He may have some Super-8 movies of campus streakers. He could even be one of the stars. Look for those movies around his house. Streaker movies are incredibly valuable now. You can sell them to Internet porn sites for thousands of dollars. With the money you make peddling your granddad's porn, you might be able to pay off an entire month's tuition at State U.

All of these activities, from gulping to stuffing to streaking, enriched the college experience. But nothing has enriched college more effectively than intercollegiate football. Football has been more important in the maturation of the American university than swallowing slithering finfish or bobbing up and down as you race across campus quadrangles in the buff. College football is king. Nothing happening on a modern university campus is as important. Well, maybe sex. But only because sex happens much more frequently than once every Saturday afternoon in the fall. No modern college could survive without sex and football. You probably wouldn't be going to State U. if it weren't for sex and football. So to keep the students coming (oops), we just concentrate on cozy co-ed cohabitation and gladiatorial games of the gridiron. Hey! It works. Party schools like State U. have learned the formula for attracting students.

Where the Boys Are---Stoned With the Girls

Another major change in focus for American colleges and universities began in the second half of the 20th century when appearance began to substitute for substance. There was the appearance of the university as the center of quiet conservative sophistication in the 1950's, when, actually, college kids were getting drunk at college football games and staging panty raids. Three-week-long spring breaks in Ft. Lauderdale became the rage of the late 50's as well as the subject of a hit movie, "Where the Boys Are," starring Connie Francis. Then, in the 1960's, the university appeared to be the center of social change. In fact, kids were just going to college football games and discovering rock-and-roll music, sex, and drugs—not necessarily in that order. With "the pill" in 1964 came the greatest sexual revolution since the time of Henry XIII. Everyone had multiple partners, but was married to no one. In 1969, Woodstock replaced the Ft. Lauderdale of Connie Francis as the place where the boys and girls are stoned. With the exception of four clean-shaven, well-dressed young men from Liverpool, every civilized male of the late 60's was as hairy as Homo erectus. (Now here's a name that explains "the rise of man," don't you think?)

Emulating their hominid ancestors--I hope you understand Cliff's fancy words--college guys grew their hair and beards four feet long so parents and draft officers couldn't recognize them in Woodstock newsreels and TV clips.

If you haven't seen a Woodstock picture of your granddad or uncle with his four-foot beard, you're really missing something. He'll keep the photo hidden in the back of his sock drawer. You should sneak into his bedroom on bowling night and look for the photo. Be sure, after splitting your gut with laughter, to put the photo right back where you found it. It has no resale value. But you could use it for blackmail if your parents refuse to let you get a tongue stud.

In the early 1970's, State U. earned a reputation as the center of anti-war protests. In fact, guys struggled full time to get away from the draft--when they weren't at college football games. To keep the draft boards forever guessing, guys let their hair and beards and sideburns grow even longer. That's why college men never got drafted. Camouflage! Finally, in the 1980's and 1990's, State U. took on a brand new appearance--that of the national center of technological innovation, business, and finance. Haircuts and shaving slowly came back into style. Seeing opportunities to get rich quick, students flocked to State U. like hordes of prospectors in the great gold rush of 1849. The Conestoga wagon of the gold rush was replaced by the red Camero and the SUV. Your granddad probably had a Conestoga wagon when he was a kid. Ask him about those good old days. He'll probably say that he still prefers the Conestoga wagon. At least, with the Conestoga wagon, the transmission was likely to last for more than one year and the mileage sure beat those gas-guzzling SUV's.

Reflecting contemporary turn-of-the-century values, economics became the most popular college major on our campus. By the way, State U. has a great economics program with two incredibly popular courses--Economics 111 (Secretly Investing Your Parents' Tuition Check On Wall Street) and Economics 213 (NASDAQ Stock Tips). I recommend both courses, especially NASDAQ Stock Tips. These days, everyone needs professional investing advice. You won't have any money to invest while still a student, but just wait until you get out. You know, once you graduate from college, you'll be making more money than you know what to do with. Just look at me. I've got money to burn. If you get a great job, like I did, you'll want to do a whole lot of investing.

Some students start investing too early—before they have much money and before they've taken a single economics course. That's why we have employers like McDonalds and Burger King—to bail out student investors. With the new student emphasis on filthy lucre, these fast food chains sprang up all over the country in the 80's and 90's, providing full-time, year-round, minimum-wage employment for college students whose portfolios had tanked. College football continued to be the favorite leisure-time activity throughout the century with beer and sex tied for second.

Chapter 5

Endless Adjustments

Follow the Ivy

Well, now that you've learned the history of higher education, it's probably time for you to settle into a regular routine at State U. Your first few days on campus will be real confusing. At orientation, an upperclassman may tell you that attending classes will help you do real good in college. An upperclassman, by the way, is a freshman who arrived on campus a week earlier than you. He or she knows everything there is to know about the place—the best bars and hangout joints, where to meet girls or guys, what fraternity to pledge, what courses give out all A's, which coin-operated washing machine starts up without coins if you kick it in just the right spot, which bookstore lets you slip out the back door without paying, and precisely how the entire universe functions. Listen up real good when upperclassmen talk. They have great advice. So what about going to class?

There is some truth to the notion you should attend classes. But classes are so huge you'll never be missed. Nobody takes roll call. Plus, these days most professors put their notes up on the Internet. If they don't, you can find students working their way through college by selling class notes and final exams. Despite these modern conveniences, you might still decide to go to class. If so, you'll need to find your way around the ivy-covered brick and granite buildings. Each building looks the same and none has a nameplate on the outside (Fig. 2.1). Nameplates disturb the ivy and detract from the mystique of college buildings. College is all about appearances, so college administrators will not let nameplates get in the way of ivy. Put the nameplate idea to rest. You need a better strategy to identify the buildings.

If you think you can navigate with the map they gave out at orientation, forget it! The map hasn't been updated in thirteen years and names of the roads and buildings have changed several times. This is because the administration must immortalize (until the next big donor comes along) the latest alumnus to contribute cash to the football program or the university president's home renovation fund (see Chapter 17).

Cliff told me that the home renovation fund is huge. He says State U. sinks millions of dollars into the president's mansion. Yet, at a Board meeting, the president told us his mansion is a wreck. He keeps calling it an embarrassment to the state, the nation, and all of western civilization (except, perhaps, Bolivia and Paraguay). He's not satisfied with the University's having renovated only forty-three rooms in the past three years. He claims much more renovation is needed to make his family comfortable.

Me and Cliff talk privately about the president's excesses; but we know we can't say anything publicly if we want to stay on the Board. Any public criticism of a university president means short tenure as a State U. administrator. Lots of other Board members know our president is a lightweight, but fear he is the best we'll ever get. They're afraid he'd leave if he ever heard criticism. Thin skin, you know. So everyone on the Board sees no evil, speaks no evil (and what's the other one? Smells no evil?). They want the president to stay until he's ninety or even ninety-five. Me and Cliff, we keep our mouths shut too.

"Who else would come to State U. with our lousy football and basketball records? Just more losers," they say. "It's tough to get a decent university president when we rank 117th out of 117 Division 1A football teams and when we have a conference record of 1 and 28 over the last few years."

Guess they have a point. But I digress. So how do you find your way to your first State U. class? Not a simple matter. Start by looking for the right building. You do this by trial and error. Early in the morning--long before the sun rises--march through campus. Walk carefully as the overnight dew on the unmowed lawn will soak through your shoes and run up your ninety-seven-yard-long pants legs (see Chapter 4). You should wander through each campus building, one-by-one, looking for the directory. Your first class will probably be in Peabody Hall. Peabody Hall is where first classes are usually held. Your hunt for Peabody Hall will take hours and, long before you're finished, the rain will start. When, to escape the rain, you finally stumble into an unnamed building that looks the way a Peabody Hall should look, search high and low for the building directory. You'll find it on the wall directly behind (and totally obscured by) a seven-foot high vending machine.

The drink menu, by the way, reflects the corporate interests of a prominent member of the university's Governing Board. This is the way we do things at State U. We reward our friends on the Governing Board. Over the past seven years, the privileged campus vendor has been SuperCola. The president of State U. granted SuperCola a monopoly on campus vending services. You'll see the SuperCola logo everywhere you go. SuperCola jingles have replaced the National Anthem at football and basketball games. This is not such a bad thing. The SuperCola jingle is a lot easier to sing than the Star Spangled Banner. Even Mariah Carey's voice sounds marginally pleasant when she does the SuperCola jingle.

The building directory, hidden by the SuperCola vending machine, will be on the third floor, right across from a departmental office. If you're lucky, the directory will give you the name of the building you're in. More than likely, it won't. So you will have to stand in line outside the office of a departmental secretary who will be making life difficult for a long line of lost freshmen. She's been giving students grief for forty-one years. She loves tormenting students, but you'll never detect pleasure from the expression on her seasoned poker face. When your turn comes around, shout out to the secretary, "Yo, lady. Whadda ya call this here building? Huh? Peabody Hall, right?" This is the correct way to phrase a question if your college is in the northeast. A northeast secretary will respond in a nasal twang, "So, what's the problem, already? You can't read a map or what?" Then she will yell out the door to a janitor lazily mopping the floor (it's been raining all morning and you're soaked to the bone), "Hey, Bert. Tell this guy where to go, O.K?"

If you're at a southern or southwestern college, you must use the word "ma'am" three times in each sentence. Never ever say "yo" or "huh." A southern secretary will refer to you as sugar or sweetie, even if you are a hulking 373-pound offensive lineman. "Lordamercy, sugar!" she'll say. "Y'all some kinda hunk, sweetie. Say, now, whatever can ah do fo y'all, now's ya come all the way up to this here third flo?"

Whether northern or southern, the secretary will only know the name of her own building. It will be Barnaby Hall, not Peabody. If it's a California secretary, she'll gently suggest you pick a building with the proper karma for that day of the week. So back you go to the random search. By the time you finally find Peabody Hall, it will be 1:45 p.m., your first four classes will be over, the rain will have turned into a monsoon, and the dining hall will have closed. It won't open for dinner until 5:30. Good time to start that diet you've been putting off for so long. Good idea unless you are a recruited 373-pound offensive lineman. In that case, you don't dare miss a meal. In fact, the coach has probably told you and all the other guys under four hundred pounds to beef up a bit if you want to stay on the team.

After all this hassle, you might think that someone would have figured out that Barnaby Hall needs a sign by the entrance. In fact, 388 written requests sit on file. Another secretary has kept a record of the work orders submitted. But hell will freeze over before a sign goes up. That's because this is a Type I problem. It's a Type I problem because the idea came from the faculty, students, and staff. That's the definition of a Type I — one initiated by a non-administrator. To resolve a Type I problem, university administrators would have to do something not their own idea. University administrators don't do things others suggest. Never! If they don't think of it themselves, they won't act upon it. Barnaby Hall will never get a sign. Neither will Peabody. But not all problems are Type I's. There's another type. Problems identified by administrators are called Type II problems. Type II problems may have absolutely no merit, but administrators will solve Type II problems almost as soon as they come up (see Chapter 21).

Attics, Basements, Barracks, and Bat Guano

Once you've recovered from your Peabody search, you'll be ready to search for Smyth Hall. That's where your second period class is held. It will be in room 417. That's in the attic of Smyth Hall, by the way. All classrooms are in one of three locations. Some are in the non-air-conditioned basements of ivy-covered buildings with noisy sewer pipes right overhead. The sewer pipes usually leak, so choose your seat with utmost care. Some are in dingy, bat-infested attics of non-air-conditioned, ivy-covered buildings, like Smyth Hall (Fig. 5.1). Watch out for the bat guano. The rest of your classes will be in non-air-conditioned, ivy-covered, termite-riddled temporary wooden structures thrown together in about a week in 1946 for returning WW II vets.

Hey Doc! Does Speling Count?

(Fig 5.1)

Here, the ivy plays a structural role. It holds up the roof. Termites love the wooden chairs almost as much as they love the support beams and rafters, so the chairs are likely to collapse. Select a chair as if you're Goldilocks in the home of the three bears. Check each chair out carefully. If you weigh 373 pounds, it's better to stand up all semester long.

    When you get to the Smyth Hall attic, you will discover a tiny pink note (spattered with brown and white bat droppings) tacked to the door of room 417 telling you that section 37 of Economics 213 (NASDAQ Stock Tips) has been combined with section 14. You are to transfer to section 14 that meets in room 311 in the third floor attic of Barnaby Hall. Oh my god! Not that same gruff secretary again! It takes you another seventeen minutes to walk across campus in the rain. It always rains in the first week of classes--even in Nevada. By the time you get to your new destination, all 632 seats in room 311, as well as the aisles and fire exits, will be filled. You will have to sit on the floor--for the rest of the semester. Your principle instructor will be a teaching assistant who appears young enough to be your daughter. She won't speak any recognizable form of English. What a way for you to begin college! Fortunately, you won't have to put up with her all semester. Occasionally a strange old professor, a Dr. Lars Sigfried Jose Ahamadahoolahanski (the students all call him Dr. "Hoola"), will show up to teach the class. But his English, it turns out, is even worse (see Chapter 17).

Rap Is Not Culture

Finding your way around campus is just the first adjustment. You will also have to learn how to get along with your five apartment roommates. Not one will share a single aspect of your own cultural, ethnic, religious, political, or philosophical background. In fact, you are each from different continents — all but Antarctica. State U. seems unable to attract any students from Antarctica despite following every Affirmative Action guideline on the books. We've been cited several times for continental discrimination and we fear loss of accreditation if we cannot attract a representative number of students from each continent. So, if you're a native of Antarctica, please apply to State U. So long as you have a valid Antarctican birth certificate, you're a shoe-in, even if you are still in third grade. We've got to meet our continental quotas.

O.K., back to roommates. The lesser assistant dean who assigns dorm and apartment rooms can't tell from first names whether your roommates are guys or gals. So you'll probably get a mixture. None of this will matter, however, because each of your roommates will like rap, hard rock, and recreational sex just as much as you do. I don't consider rap and hard rock to be part of culture, by the way. Neither does the chairman of the State U. music department who's a world authority on modern music. In his critically acclaimed treatise, "The Authoritative Classification of Modern Music," he places rap and hard rock together in a chapter he calls "Aesthetically Vacuous Vibrational Emissions." What a mouthful! Like all professors, he writes stuff that's way too highbrow, but I sort of get his point.

So keep away from me (and the whole music department) if you're going to play that noise you call music. But recreational sex, well, that's another matter. If you're talking the sex stuff — hey! I'm available. (Call me at work, not at home, O.K.) Your roommates will enjoy sitting around with you all day watching MTV. MTV isn't culture either, but it will help you pass the time as you eagerly await the season's first football game. Now, football, that's what I call culture. However, your roommates expect the game to involve kicking a round ball instead of the strange one Americans use. They won't be prepared for the calculated mayhem of the American game. That's culture shock.

Only 45 Amps? Come On!

Speaking of shock, you'll face countless other challenges, like trying to hook up your stereo system and computer by yourself. Remember, you won't have Dad's help. Almost immediately, you'll run into a major problem. Your campus apartment will have only 45 amps of electrical service. Why don't they say this in the college catalog? The State U. catalog says nothing about apartment amperage. The Board has been trying to change this for years. But the president says it's undignified to list apartment amperage in the catalog. What a pain he is! Your forty-eight-inch sub-woofers each draw 30 amps and you brought all twelve. When you get all wired up in that underpowered apartment, you can't even see the walls vibrating. Back home, your system cracked the plaster in the house and brought down your sister's bedroom ceiling three times. That's what brothers are for — keeping sisters on their toes. No way you'll get this kind of performance from a wimpy 45 amps. Fortunately, there are twelve other students in your complex who didn't bring sub-woofers. They let you run 60-amp cables down the hallways from each of their apartments so you get the power you need. What good would your system be if you couldn't see the walls vibrate?

Salmonella Surprise

Problems don't stop with the stereo system. To save money, you'll need to find a store selling used textbooks with discounts greater than 5 percent. Lots of luck! You will also have to search all over campus for a place with edible food. This will take effort. The campus food center at my old alma mater served a twenty-five-cent entree we called Salmonella surprise. Salmonella surprise is a sort of goulash made from last week's unsold food. It was surprisingly tasty. However, five times in one year the Salmonella surprise landed me in the campus infirmary. After the fifth lengthy stay in the infirmary, I stopped buying the Salmonella surprise. I really hated to spend the extra money, but I gave in and started buying fresh cafeteria entrees for fifty cents each.

Oh! No! Not the Health Center

Whatever you do, don't get sick at a university! The modern day student health center offers no treatment for Salmonella infections. They won't treat colds, flu, cuts, bruises, sprains, migraines, asthma, or broken bones either, unless you are a jock. Athletes get unlimited 24/7 medical benefits. But the jockless among you get no decent medical service at the university. What's the health center for? Is it just for supporting the jocks? No! It's for research on sexually transmitted diseases (STD's). Don't I know about STD's! When I was a student, the State U. health center got me out of a whole lot of trouble with those pesky STD bugs. I lived on penicillin for a whole semester and I had to change girlfriends almost every week.

So just what happens if you should ignore my advice and decide to stumble into the health center? When you arrive with an upper respiratory infection and a raging fever, a matronly person in a white coat will thrust a clipboard at you, saying something in a language you won't understand. "Do kvestion," she might say. If you ask for clarification, she will repeat, "Do kvestion."

There will be many questions. If fact, you will have to answer seventy-five embarrassing questions, each involving intimate details of your personal sex life. There will be no empty seats, so you'll have to fill out the questionnaire standing up. Everyone in the waiting room will remember the questionnaire. The whole time you're filling it out, they'll be looking over your shoulder to see what you put down for question thirty-seven. Number thirty-seven is a doosie! When you finally get to see a doctor, he will be convinced you acquired your cold through some unnatural act. Don't bother trying to tell him otherwise. He won't believe you. If you ever want to be treated at the student health center, you better make up your mind right now that every college ailment is sexually transmitted. Even poison ivy is sexually transmitted. This is no joke! There's a whole research team at the State U. medical school working on sexually transmitted poison ivy. But poison ivy is just the beginning. Many other common diseases are sexually transmitted. Rabies is sexually transmitted. So are nasal polyps, athlete's foot, ear infections, and buck teeth. My advice? Stay away from the health center, particularly if you are sick.

So, having dealt with about 187 similar problems of equal urgency, you will now be ready, in the sixth week of your first semester, to consider attending classes on a regular basis.

SECTION III

OFF TO A REAL GOOD START

CHAPTER 6

CHOOSING A COMPUTER

The Cyber Professor

Universities have become computerized in the past two decades. One of the first educational products of the computer era is the computerized SAT test (named after the day of the week it's always given). All the SAT questions are now written by computer—just like college tests. You need to take the SAT if you want to go to college. This is how colleges find out if you're smart. But someone in China or Korea is putting all the SAT questions on the Internet. So, if you study these Internet questions, you'll appear smart even if you're a dummy. When I took the SAT, nobody knew the questions in advance, so it was real hard. You really had to be smart back then. I got a combined score of 714. I remember this number 'cause that's how many homeruns Babe Ruth got. Well, 714 is a big number, so I guess the State U. admissions officers could tell how smart I am. I bet "The Babe" didn't do as good as me on the SAT.

Today, computers do everything. They admit you to college and they register you for classes. They create and grade your multiple-choice college exams and they mail you your grades. They alphabetize your name for graduation where you are handed a computer-generated diploma on a fake sheepskin. If you commute to college, it's the computer in your brand new red Saturn convertible that gets you there. It's also a computer that controls your mobile ghetto blaster to keep you (and everyone else within a six-county radius) entertained with rap as you drive to school.

The courses you take are presented in so-called SMART[3] classrooms with computerized audio-visual equipment. Thrust into these SMART classrooms are graying professors who've been teaching the same boring material for thirty years using only cheap, squeaky chalk (full of sand and little bits of gravel). The professor reads from a faded scratch pad full of dog-eared notes, occasionally pausing to tell a convoluted, anachronistic (Cliff again) joke that nobody thinks is funny. Your professor will look up from the scratch pad once in a while, glancing nervously at the computer with which he shares the podium. He's been told by the dean to start using the SMART equipment because the university spent so much money buying and installing it. He'll ineptly fumble around with the SMART equipment hoping for a student to show him how the damn stuff works. If you're in one of those classes, let the guy struggle for a while. It will be hilarious. Then, if you know any electronics, get up there and end the torture. You'll make a friend for life.

It's smart to make friends with your professors. Professors write reference letters for your medical school applications. You'll want live professors doing your letters, not cyber professors. As computerized instruction progresses, live professors may vanish, showing up only in cyber space (on classroom TV's or instructional CD's). Cyber professors are a bit stiff and they don't write letters too good. So, if you get a live professor in a class, bond right away (see Chapter 7). It could be your last chance to bond with a live professor. Except for med school reference letters, who cares about live professors? Nobody really pays attention to professors, anyhow.

Dean of Student Computer Purchasing

Unless you want to do a whole lot of real hard work in college, you'll need your own personal computer. You should not, however, buy your own PC until a university computer has admitted you to college and your parents' computer has accepted on your behalf. Each university has different computer-purchasing recommendations you must follow. This is because

---

[3] SMART stands for "So Much Automation Ruins Teaching"

every university has a different corporate businessperson in the computer industry on its Governing Board. At State U. there are two such people. One is Phyllis (the same Phyllis who likes feminine mascots). She represents her employer's interests in computer hardware. The other is Alvin, who's on the Board to push his company's interests in computer software. Neither one knows, or cares to know, anything about education at State U. The Board members' parents eased them through the state's premier private university twenty miles down the road. Me and Cliff, we aren't like this. No stuck-up private universities for us. We're State U. threw and threw.

Those other Governing Board members say they represent State U. out of the deep sense of civic duty they learned at that private university. Don't believe a word of it. To them, a deep sense of civic duty means special rewards. Lots of favors, extra special treatments, and loads of free NFL and NBA tickets for starters. They pretend to be fine, dedicated citizens able to run State U. by showing up on campus a couple of hours each month. They're full of it! They don't run anything at State U. Well, they run up the catering bills. Those bills must be huge. I've never had such fancy meals. So these other people stay on the Board just because they like gourmet food, executive power, and great perks.

As a State U. student, whether you like it or not, you'll need to deal with the Governing Board. That's because a State U. computer will invest a big chunk of your tuition payment into the corporate portfolios of these Governing Board members. So it makes sense to follow the university's official recommendations about buying a computer. If you are still unsure about computer purchasing, consult with the Dean of Student Computer Purchasing (DSCP). The DSCP won't know anything about computers, but will know which company to recommend. It is no accident that the DSCP is appointed directly by the president of the Governing Board and plays bridge each week with the snooty members of the Board.

No Need for That Webster Book

Just as important as your computer is your software selection. You must have Spell Check. You learned how to spell way back in the second, third, and fourth grades. For something as boring as speling, you shouldn't have to rely upon your memory. Nor should you have to rely on that heavy Webster book your Aunt Grace gave you for elementary school graduation. You may not even know how to use a Webster book. Chances are you've used it only to press and preserve leaves for a seventh grade science project or, if you're a girl, to preserve all the dance and prom corsages you've collected.

Even if you knew how to look stuff up in the Webster book, you cannot read anything now. The pages are all covered with green or pink stains from leaves or flowers. Better leave the Webster book home with all the leaves among the leaves. Well, leave it home unless you want to do a senior honors project. Then you'll need a Webster book (see Chapter 15). Otherwise, forget the Webster book. Be modern. Get Spell Check. Everyone in college uses a speling chequer. As always, consult your Dean of Student Computer Purchasing if you are even slightly in doubt as to which software package to buy.

Owed to a Spell Chequer!

Until you have used a computerized speling chequer, you will have no idea how useful it can be. Here in Table 6.1 is an example of how a speling chequer can make a masterpiece out of gibberish. This example comes from a student's final paper in English 423, Advanced Poetic Composition.

TABLE 6.1:
OWED TO A SPELL CHEQUER

> Eye have a speling chequer
> It came with my pea sea
> It plainly marques four my revue
> Miss steaks eye kin knot sea.
> Eye strike a key and type a word
> And weight four it two say
> Weather eye am wrong oar write
> It shows me strait a weigh.
> As soon as a mist ache is maid
> It nose bee fore two long
> And eye can put the error rite
> Its rare lea ever wrong.
> Eye have run this poem threw it
> I am shore your pleased two no
> Its letter perfect awl the weigh
> My chequer tolled me sew.

This example proves how useful speling chequers can be. Imagine trying to do this poem without the help of a computer. Out of the question!

When Humerus is just Not Funny

If I had Spell Check when I was a high school junior, I wouldn't have gotten a score of minus twelve on a ten-point question in third period English. You may not believe it, but personal computers did not exist back then. We used a thing called an abacus. It ran without batteries, but it had no speling chequer. With Spell Check, I would have known to use the word humorous, instead of humerus, on my ten-point English essay question. You see, I had just come from Mr. Szalay's second period zoology class where we had been dissecting the front limb of a cat. I had learned the name of the major arm bone of mammals--the humerus. I had the zoology speling in mind when, in the very next period, I answered the English essay question. I wrote humerus instead of humorous. My third period English teacher gave me minus ten for getting her question wrong and minus two for misspeling humorous in the process. This is the only time in my life that I've gotten less than zero on a school assignment. At the time, I saw nothing funny about this incident and I still don't think it was humerus.

Random Word Generators

The most useful computer software package by far is the random word generator, one of which is manufactured by MicroSmooth under the brand name RandGen. It sells for $59.95 in most computer stores (Fig 6.1).

The strength of the random word generator is that it removes the human element from sentence and paragraph construction. This is similar to the way voting machines cut out the human element in Florida ballot counting in the 2000 presidential election. Machines never make mistakes. Computers are no exception. So, with RandGen, just a few simple keystrokes enable you to do real good at writing professional-looking term papers, book reviews, and essays.

You simply select the subject (Moby Dick book report, for example), the number of pages required for the report (twelve pages, let's say), and the average number of words per sentence (seventeen is a good choice). The software package arranges words into sentences and paragraphs and gives you the entire report in the time it takes a laser printer to do two hard copies. One copy is for you to turn in to your professor when the assignment is due (in the next two minutes). The other is for you to keep for your fraternity or

(Fig. 6.1)

sorority files.

To give you an idea of the power of RandGen, Table 6.2 reproduces a short essay on an Agatha Christie novel. The essay was submitted by a college senior taking a course in the critical review of modern literature, English 449 (Evolution of the Modern Mystery Novel). The English professor rated this student's essay as one of the finest short reviews she had seen in the academic year. "The students who have access to RandGen are at a remarkable advantage over those who still compose their reports and essays by themselves," reported Professor Doubting. "Work like this was simply beyond the reach of most of my students back in 1997, before RandGen made its breakthrough onto the college scene."

TABLE 6.2:
A SHORT ESSAY CREATED BY MICROSMOOTH'S "RANDGEN,"
A STATE-OF-THE-ART RANDOM WORD GENERATOR

> Its are job to solve crimes and other things? Upon entering the house in as much as the Butler was responsible for doing it. The house was red! In addition and in fact; a knife was found near the Rope close to the revolver. Obviously it was used to commit the crime? this phenomena is Often. But its a data we dont know the cause of. It!

The essay in Table 6.2 does suffer from some minor capitalization and punctuation problems. But these are easily corrected with two upgrade programs. Several manufacturers of random word generators also make random capitalization generators and random punctuation generators. Each is sold separately. Again, check with your Dean of Student Computer Purchasing before investing. MicroSmooth versions, RandCap and RandPunk, each sell for about $39.95.

It is not much good to have a computer select your words if the program does not know which words to capitalize and what types of punctuation to utilize and where. RandCap and RandPunk eliminate the guesswork of capitalization and punctuation much as RandGen eliminates guesswork of word selection. As an added feature, the most recent version of RandGen-- RandGen Post-Millennium Edition--inserts weighty expressions such as "in fact" and "in as much as" throughout your reports. The use of such expressions impresses college professors and is sure to get you in real good with them.

I recommend your purchasing a set of all three software packages (or competitive brand, depending upon your Governing Board representative). You'll find you use them in just about every whole-sentence class.

The Noun-Adjective Enrichment Problem

In creating RandGen Post-Millennium Edition, MicroSmooth has also corrected a minor unanticipated defect in its earlier version of the random word generator--the so-called "noun-adjective enrichment problem." The English language, it turns out, has too many nouns and adjectives. This leaves a gaping deficiency in other parts of speech including verbs, adverbs, prepositions, pronouns, and conjunctions. Earlier versions of MicroSmooth's random word generator tend to combine parts of speech into sentences based upon their Webster-book frequencies. This results in sentences short of verbs, adverbs, prepositions, pronouns, and conjunctions. Sentences are much more readable when they contain a rich assortment of the various parts of speech. Verbs, in particular, are considered quite useful. So are expletives, but not in polite company. Expletives are reserved for transcripts of office voice recordings by U. S. presidents.

MicroSmooth did not intend RandGen to create a glut of verbless, adverbless, prepositionless, pronounless, and conjunctionless sentences. It was simply a computer programming oversight. When it released RandGen Post-Millennium Edition in February of 2003, MicroSmooth corrected the glitch by augmenting, by a factor of 6.38, the frequencies of all verbs in its database. Adverbs, prepositions, and conjunctions got frequency augmentation factors of 8.69, 14.83, and 22.33 respectively. Pronouns got boosted by a factor of 4.72. All this extra work drove up the price to $69.95, but upgrading with RandGen Post-Millennium Edition is well worth the additional few dollars. The performance of RandGen Post-Millennium Edition is impressive. One college junior who requested anonymity wrote this to me:

> I was abel to produse a 38-page assay on the stuff of Henery David Thouough in only about three minutes with my new RandGen Post-Millennium Edition. You can do real good with that program; like, you know, I got an A on my Thouough thing and it was real easy. But, I need a new printer. Mine is to slow and stuff like that.

A professor of history at a large northeastern state university commented that he is starting to see, for the first time in more than a decade, readable reports from his junior/senior students in History 338 (Modern European History). He writes:

> I am impressed with the quality of the work I see coming from RandGen Post-Millennium Edition. I am pleased that our Dean of Student Computer Purchasing and our State U. Board of Governors have so strongly encouraged students to purchase this outstanding random word generator. RandGen Post-Millennium Edition does amazing things, and, what's more, it is one hundred percent compatible with my new MicroSmooth Report Grader. I require my students to submit their reports and essays on diskettes. Then I simply pop each disk into my office PC. Seconds later my MicroSmooth Report Grader program has the student's report fully corrected. Report Grader then prints out the grade for each student, having already made adjustments according to the University Presidents' Standard Grading Curve. (See Chapter 11) Were it not for the far-sighted leadership of our university president and the Governing Board who chose MicroSmooth as the official and exclusive university software provider, our students would still be writing their own reports and we would still be grading them, ourselves.

Finest Football Players Money Can Buy

The most exciting chapter in this story is that MicroSmooth now subsidizes the State U. intercollegiate athletics program. With its huge annual donations, MicroSmooth has helped us attract a big-name football coach. We have expanded the football stadium by fifty percent and built a domed practice field. MicroSmooth's donations have partially funded an automated, 127-unit, closed circuit TV system that monitors, by satellite, all major college football games throughout the country. Recruiting, too, has gotten a huge boost. In the past year alone, our head football coach has recruited eighty of the finest college football players money can buy. Everyone is looking forward to a winning football team. It has been too many years without a victory.

Chapter 7

Hector's Hints to Get in Real Good with Your Professors

Excellent, Provocative, Thoughtful Questions

To do real good in college, you need to bond with your professors. Whether consciously or subconsciously, professors give higher grades to students who successfully bond with them. If you're a real hot co-ed there's a sure-fire bonding technique that always works, but let's not go there, O.K? The second best bonding technique is asking excellent, provocative, thoughtful questions in class. I recommend your doing this on the first day of class, preferably in the first minute. Use the interlude between the professor's announcing the course title and his or her first mention of course content. Just blurt out your excellent, provocative, thoughtful questions as soon as the professor stops writing the title of the course on the blackboard. Say you're in the most popular course at State U., NASDAQ Stock Tips. This class is always jammed, so, to be recognized, you must be quick and persistent. Other NASDAQ students will attempt to bond at the very same time. Competition is keen, especially in popular courses like NASDAQ Stock Tips.

There are many appropriate questions, so you need to consider ones most likely to get you in real good with your professor. Table 7.1 lists a few excellent, provocative, thoughtful questions guaranteed to leave a terrific impression on your professor. These are exactly the questions you should ask. Don't feel limited to one or two questions. Ask as many as you can. As soon as the title of the course goes up on the board, ask maybe a dozen rapid-fire questions. Continue doing this throughout the first week or two of classes. By asking scads of questions early in the semester, you'll make an impression that could last the entire term. This is a great bonding strategy. If you bond with your professor this way, he or she will cheerfully write outstanding reference letters for your medical school applications. If your class is in a huge lecture room, like Barnaby Hall room 311, the professor will find it hard to get to know you among the other 632 students. Asking lots of excellent, provocative, thoughtful questions is especially important in very large classes. You can reuse the list in Table 7.1 about ten times before a professor will notice repetition. Afterwards, you should start making up your own personal questions. Just remember, they must be excellent, provocative, and thoughtful. It's probably a good idea to memorize Table 7.1 at this very moment, while it's fresh in your mind. That way your bonding can begin right away and you'll beat out all those other pushy students.

Hey, Doc!

Begin each of your excellent, provocative, thoughtful questions with a friendly, courteous appellation. (Watch out! This word, "appellation," is not the same as that big mountain range in Virginia. The Virginia mountain range starts with a capital A and ends up somewhere in central Georgia.) I recommend the simple appellation, "Hey, Doc." "Hey, Doc" is short, gender neutral, and informal enough for today's more laid-back classroom style. Furthermore, it says you know your professor has a Ph.D. Professors are impressed when you publicly acknowledge their degrees. So turn to Table 7.1 right now and start memorizing. You'll thank me for this advice.

TABLE 7.1:
HECTOR'S EXCELLENT, PROVOCATIVE QUESTIONS TO ASK IN THE FIRST MINUTE OF CLASS

1. Hey, Doc! Do we have tests in here or what?
2. Hey, Doc! What's gonna be on the first test?
3. Hey, Doc! Do we hafta read the book?
4. Hey, Doc! Does the stuff in class count?
5. Hey, Doc! If you do problems and stuff on the blackboard, do we have to learn it?
6. Hey, Doc! My roommate took this course last year and said it was real easy. He didn't study a lick and he got an A. He just played guitar in the room all day and he had this real cute chick, too. Is your course still this easy?
7. Hey, Doc! Everybody says this course is real boring and nobody ever shows up. Are they right?
8. Hey, Doc! Do I need a calculator for the test?
9. Hey, Doc! Why do I need to take NASDAQ? I'm gonna be a doctor, not a Wall Street geek. You just need stuff like biology and such for medical school. Right?
10. Hey, Doc! Does speling count?
11. Hey, Doc! Do we hafta write whole sentences in NASDAQ? We did this once in Comp. 101.
12. Hey, Doc! You use the same test every year, right?
13. Hey, Doc! I missed the first four classes. Did you talk about anything important?*

* You shouldn't ask this particular question on the first day of classes. It's better to wait until the fifth class meeting for this one.

Chapter 8

Modular Answers to Test Questions

Hector's Balderdash Approach

The computer age has ushered in a new style of college test taking. The test questions haven't changed much in the past ten or twenty years. But the way students answer them has changed big time. The new style involves the use of modular answers. I call it the modular approach or, more properly, the Balderdash approach. This is my original idea. I figured the whole thing out myself. No joke. But it was stupid of me not to patent the idea. I kick myself every time I think how much money I've lost. But my loss is your gain. The Balderdash approach is simple but elegant. So, here's how it goes.

First, you memorize a long list of potential answers to test questions. Don't concern yourself with the questions. Just learn a lot of real good answers. A computer searches its memory bank for answers. You should do the same thing. Then, when questions appear on a test, you simply plug in an answer from your memory bank--any answer that sounds right. The procedure is similar to that of the old parlor game, Dictionary, now marketed under the trade name of Balderdash. In Balderdash, players make up definitions that sound right for a word nobody at the table has ever heard.

Take the word "syzygy." Syzygy could be defined in Balderdash as a large, densely populated island off the coast of Italy. This is because syzygy sounds a whole lot like Sicily (except for the capital letter S at the beginning; the capital letter makes Sicily sound a whole lot more important than syzygy). I've won about twelve games of Balderdash just because I know about syzygy and because I learned to pronounce syzygy just like an Italian would. To use the modular approach, just follow this example. Take all your tests as if you were playing a game of Balderdash. Pick whatever sounds right. This really works. But you need to know lots of real good answers.

Table 8.1 is a good place to start. I know what I am saying. I did a computer search of the correct answers to test questions asked at 197 U.S. colleges and universities over the past decade. The twenty-six answers that come up most frequently are listed right here in Table 8.1 — most frequent answer first. So Table 8.1 is the best list anywhere. You should memorize this table. Do it right away. If you memorize ten or twelve additional lists like this one, then you can answer any question your professor is likely to ask. When you're not too sure of your answer, pretend you're a pre-med learning how to write prescriptions as a doctor does. Make every letter illegible. Almost always you will be given the benefit of the doubt.

TABLE 8.1:
HECTOR'S EXCELLENT MODULAR ANSWERS TO COLLEGE TEST QUESTIONS

1. CUBIC ZIRCONIUM
2. 1066
3. $\pi r^2 h$
4. EQUILATERAL
5. NATIVE AMERICANS
6. 186,000 MILES PER SECOND
7. THE FALL OF ROME
8. ANTIMATTER
9. THE BEER-LAMBERT LAW
10. CHARLES DARWIN
11. OPERANT CONDITIONING
12. THE INCLINED PLANE
13. NEO-CLASSICISM
14. NEO-NAZIISM
15. NEOLITHIC
16. NEODYMIUM
17. NEON
18. KNEE
19. KNEED
20. THNEED (FROM "THE LORAX," BY DR. SEUSS)
21. CUBISM
22. IMPRESSIONISM
23. EXHIBITIONISM
24. POINTALISM
25. THE SALT OF THE EARTH
26. TWELVE

Real College Questions, Revealed

By now you should have memorized Table 8.1. I'll give you one more minute. O.K? So, without looking, see if you can use your recall of Table 8.1 to do real good on a physics test question. This question is taken directly from an actual test in introductory college physics at State U. Try your luck. No peeking at the list.

Hey Doc! Does Speling Count?

Calculate the volume of a hexagonally close-packed cubic crystal of sodium chloride that measures two angstroms on a side.

Remember, no looking back. I'll walk you through the logical procedure. Ready? O.K. Right off the bat you might be tempted to select 1066 because this answer is near the top of the list and because it has numbers in it. In fact, it has four numbers: one, zero, and two sixes. Because a cube is related to a square and a square has four sides, 1066, with its four numbers, looks real good as an answer. Yes, this is a good guess, but, unfortunately, 1066 is not the right answer.

Next try $\pi r^2 h$ because anything in physics needs a π in it somewhere, or so you'd think. Wrong again, but an excellent try. "Equilateral" seems an acceptable answer because cubes have sides of equal length. But there is something missing--numbers. After a few seconds, you should realize that the only good answer is "cubic zirconium" (because it has cubic in the answer). But watch out for "cubism." This one sounds real good too. But it's wrong. Nice try. Sodium chloride is chemical for salt. So you could easily be fooled by the "salt of the earth."

Be careful. The Balderdash approach can be tricky. But its big advantage is allowing you to breeze through an exam without thinking. No thinking is required before an exam. No thinking is required during an exam. In fact, had you done any thinking on this question, you never could have come up with "cubic zirconium" as the correct answer. Effortless selection of answers is the beauty of the modular approach. Let's try another example--this one from a humanities test on modern French painting. Here is the actual test question (no looking back, remember):

What do you call the style of a modern French painter whose pastel landscapes are best exhibited from a moderately long distance (20-40 feet)?

Here the answer is given away in the question (because of the word exhibited). This painter is obviously adhering to an artistic style known as exhibitionism. See how easy this is? Now go get your A's in every class!

Chapter 9

Beating the M/C System

Cyber Freedom, Cyber Court, and the M/C Test

Multiple-choice questions are the most common type in American college exams. This is why I told you to practice your M/C letters in high school (see Chapter 3). Have you started yet? What are you waiting for? So why are M/C tests common? Because they can be generated by computer, graded by machine, and tallied in a spreadsheet with automatic ranking by a computer. The student gets by without thinking and the professor gets by without doing any work.

Professors get no credit for teaching students, so they teach computers instead. They get all kinds of credit for teaching computers. They program electronic testing and grading systems, design distance learning courses, create virtual classrooms and, in effect, find innovative ways to phase out their own jobs (see Chapter 6). Professors who teach computers instead of students get new research equipment, new hardware and software, promotions, pay raises, and a yearlong, all-expense-paid Microsmooth fellowships to a clothing-optional resort on the French Riviera. However, upon returning from France, they discover they've been fired (replaced by their own impersonal, distance learning systems). Even more insulting is the discovery, when they return to the States, that moths have eaten their clothes while they were frolicking naked on the beaches of France.

The State U. administration loves computer-generated and computer-graded M/C tests. Computers are a lot cheaper than professors—even cheaper than the discount professors who risk their lives traveling across the Pacific Ocean in rickety old wooden boats (like the "In Roco Palentis") just to teach classes in their native tongues to American college students who can't understand a word they say (Fig. 3.2).

Despite having imported a bunch of discount professors, the State U. administration is now busy replacing them with computers. Further cost savings is one reason. Another is that administrators find it easier to deal with computers than with professors. For example, administrators can easily retire a bunch of outdated computers to Surplus Properties. That's no big deal. Computers don't mind having their cables, printers, and monitors dismembered and scattered about. They don't mind being stacked twelve-deep on dusty shelves in leaky old wooden buildings on the outskirts of campus and then forgotten for decades. But professors don't like being treated this way by administrators (especially the thing about dismemberment). So administrators have a hard time retiring outdated professors--particularly unionized professors.

To make matters worse, there are students who complain to administrators about being graded unfairly by their professors. When an administrator acts as judge and jury in a messy grade-change case, he or she could be tied up for months. Let's say a student fusses about the grading of an M/C test. If a professor wrote the M/C questions and then did the grading, an administrator might have a tough time dealing with the student's complaint. But if a computer generated each test question and if a computer did the grading and then posted the test results on the Internet, the dean will have no trouble handling the complaint. The college dean just says to the student, "Sorry kid. Everything in this course was done by computers. There can't hardly be no mistakes."

Administrators also like computers because computers don't tie them up in endless grievance hearings and mediation sessions like professors do. While many professors are militant and overly litigious, computers, by their very nature, are gentle and administration-friendly. They never force administrators to make decisions and they never hold administrators accountable for those decisions. Computers never file nasty grievances against the administration about improper or illegal infringement upon their cyber freedom.

Not so with professors. Professors are always filing grievances against the administration and dragging them into arbitration hearings. The thing a college administrator hates most, even more than making a careful and reasonable decision, is having to appear before an arbitrator or a mediator to defend one bonehead administrative move after another. Usually they squirm out of such meetings. Instead of showing up in person, administrators send a few dozen lackey-lawyers with no knowledge of the situation. The lackey-lawyers procrastinate, deceive, and lie about the facts of the case—sometimes for decades—so the administrator never goes to court, cases never get resolved, and the administrator is free to make even more bonehead decisions.

Despite the protection of lackey-lawyers, college administrators think they have tough professional lives. They try to boss around the professors. But the professors resist. For some silly reason, professors feel they have rights. Of course, they don't have any rights, but they behave as if they do.

Computers are different. Computers are easy. Computers have no rights and they know it. So computers never fight back. Best of all for administrators, there are no reactionary computer unions representing abused and downtrodden computers in cyber court.

Tricky

Computer-generated, multiple-choice tests, more than any other type, are best attacked with my modular answer strategy. Just memorize a bunch of good answers and put down the ones that sound best (see Chapter 8). But computers write M/C tests that are real tricky. The questions force you to make loads of mistakes. But, if you can just get through the computer's trickiness, you'll do real good on M/C tests. Follow my advice. I can show you how to avoid most of the usual pitfalls. I figured everything out when I was in college. It's all here in Table 9.1. Well, Table 9.1 is a bit different from the first one I made up. It's new and improved. Each year I go over the table, update it, and refine it until now it is just about perfect. So memorize Table 9.1 and you'll never have to worry about a single college M/C test.

TABLE 9.1:
HECTOR'S HELPFUL HINTS ON HOW TO DO REAL GOOD ON MULTIPLE-CHOICE TESTS IN COLLEGE

1. The longest answer is always correct unless one of the other answers is shorter.
2. The shortest answer is always wrong unless one of the other answers is longer.
3. Never pick "All of the above" unless it is preceded by "None of the above."
4. Answers containing superlatives (greatest, never, always) are always incorrect unless two or more opposite superlatives appear in the same answer. Take the example "It was the best of times. It was the worst of times." If this phrase appears as an M/C choice, you must always select it. It has opposite superlatives (best and worst) together in the same answer. It has to be the correct choice. Never forget this tip, because it is always right.
5. Answers like "B and C, but not C" are meant to trick you. They are often wrong choices. When you see answers like this one, just pick D.
6. If each question has five possible answers, you must eliminate one incorrect answer to score twenty-five percent. On some tests, that's pretty good (see Chapter 10). In a few classes, though, twenty-five percent may not be an A. In such cases, it's advisable to eliminate four incorrect answers. If you eliminate four incorrect answers, the fifth one might just be correct. But if you consistently eliminate all five answers, you are doing something wrong and you're sure to get a zero. You can't get an A with a score of zero. Even in Physical Chemistry you need scores just a tiny bit higher than zero percent to get an A. So if you keep getting zero percent on every test, you probably won't graduate. No big deal. You can drop out of college and take up an honest trade. Do you like making street-fair jewelry out of mutilated coins? This is not a bad life for a college dropout.
7. Never pick E. The test-writing computer always runs out of steam by answer D and will put something stupid as last choice (next to the letter E). Regis Philbin, host of the TV quiz show "Who Wants To Be A Millionaire?" always inserts a dumb answer as his last choice too. But his TV program only gives four choices, not five. Having five possible answers is much harder. Now you know how college differs from a TV quiz show. College sticks you with an extra choice and the professor won't give you a lifeline to ask the audience for help. Nor will he let you call your brilliant great uncle, Henry, in Saskatoon, Saskatchewan, who happens to be sitting right next to the phone and is ready to pick up on the first ring.
8. Don't forget to write your name at the top of the page. It's good practice for your composition skills to write whole words like your name once in a while just in case you have a test that is not multiple-choice.

William W. Ward

Hector's Hints on Doing Word Problems

As I've already indicated, nearly all college tests are multiple-choice. For these exams, all you need to understand are the letters A, B, C, D, and E. But sometimes, tests will sort of try to make you think. The word-problem test in science courses is just this type. Thinking is real encouraged on word-problem tests in science. But don't panic. Nobody ever thinks in college classes—especially during tests.

Just about every student at State U., even some non-science students, can do number problems. These are ones without any words. Most can multiply 2 X 3 and come up with 6. They can even do it without a pocket calculator. Those with calculators, however, do much better because they get lots of significant figures. So they multiply 2 X 3 and come up with 6.00000000. They would take it past nine significant figures, but that's as far as the calculator screen will go.

The same students can even figure out that 40/100 X 4 equals 1.60000000. But, it takes them a whole lab period to figure out how many milliliters of water must be added to 40 milliliters of a 4.0 molar salt solution to generate 100 milliliters of 1.6 molar salt solution. This kind of problem is real hard because it is a word problem. Without all the words, the problem would just be 40/100 X 4 = 1.60000000 and so you'd have to add 60 milliliters of water.

Most professors who teach lab courses (in some erotic Eastern language, of course) require no more than one word problem per hour. So you might ask, "How many word problems could a student do in a three-period lab class?" The answer is 4.66666667 word problems. How did I get this number? Easy! If the standard class period is eighty minutes long, then a three-period lab lasts 3 X 80 minutes, or 240 minutes. But there are twenty-minute-long class change periods. With two class-change periods among the three standard periods the total time is 280 minutes. Divide this by sixty minutes per hour and you get 4.66666667 hours.

Please, don't let this little exercise scare you. Never, in college, will you have to do a word problem as hard as this one. Even if your major is tough, like Indiscreet Algebras, Astrophonics, or Planting Wierd Shrubs Over Smelly Old Landfills, your word problems will always be real easy. They'll be like this word problem from Math X(1/X)—Achieving Cosmic Singularity by Multiplying Reciprocals (see Chapter 3): "Excluding the spare, calculate the number of tires on a four-wheel vehicle." The answer, of course, is 4.00000000 wheels. Professors know better than to push today's students any harder than this.

It's Too Deep

College professors allow students to report all the figures that a calculator or computer can generate. It is just too frustrating for professors to explain the concept of rounding off to the nearest significant digit. It's too deep. (This is especially true, now that Pi has been carried out to one trillion places without a single repeat.) So, whether it's 4.7 hours or 4.66666667 hours, a standard three-period lab class has time for just four word problems (plus, for the hopelessly addicted, 2.00000000 breaks for cigarettes—or for those non-tobacco, hippie-type, self-rolled things). This is why science labs take so long. You can only do four word problems in 4.66666667 hours and chances are that you will get 95.0000000 percent of the word problems flat-out wrong.

But, because almost everybody gets everything wrong in college lab classes, you basically must show up for 4.66666667 hours each week. In biology labs you mess around with a few test tubes or a fetal pig or a bunch of mutant fruit flies that escape all over the building and then lay hundreds of eggs in all the secretaries' lunches. If it's a physics lab, you play with a fresnel lens or an electrical incapacitator or a reclined plane or something like that. If it's a chemistry lab you just blow things up. Near the end of the lab period you do all the word problems, get them all wrong, and then leave. Even the jocks can meet this challenge. Plus, unless you get more than 96.6666667% of everything wrong in your lab class, you'll still pass. The University Presidents' Standard Grading Curve (see Chapter 11) guarantees that all but the bottom 3.33333333% will pass every course. You'll like college real good.

Chapter 10

Origin of the Grading Curve

Once you struggle through the first round of major exams, you'll notice that raw scores on college tests are usually low. Real low! You're not going to get ninety-eight percent or higher like you did in high school. No way! Instead, you'll get scores like thirty-seven and twenty-six. This may come as a bit of a shock to you. Decades ago, test scores as low as these could get you kicked out of college--unless your father was filthy rich or your mother was having an affair with the head of the alumni association. With grades like these, you could be out on your tush before you discovered where half of your classes meet. But times have changed. Now a score of twenty-six percent is not that bad. Why? Because of a wonderful invention called the curve. (See Chapter 11 for more information on the curve.) These days you may earn an A+ for a score of twenty-six percent in physical chemistry. A twenty-six may even earn you a special commendation by the department chairperson and a personal recommendation to skip your last two years at State U. to join the faculty at Cal Tech as a full professor of Astrophonics or Indiscreet Algebras. Why? Thanks to the curve.

The Curve Lets Everyone Do Good

How did the curve get started? You need to hear the story. Back in 1968, the presidents of three small, financially-struggling liberal arts colleges in Detroit, Cleveland, and Newark got together in the West Indies at a plush casino they jointly owned. There, they invented the curve. As the story goes, three mangoes came up together on a slot machine window and the idea hit them simultaneously. "We need a curve," they all shouted.

And so the curve was born. The curve was the presidents' way to retain the few students who actually wanted to attend college in those cities. The plan was to make it so easy for students to pass every course that none of the registered students would ever flunk out. The plan worked better than anyone expected. All students stayed in college. The invention was so special that the three presidents got free trips to Stockholm for some kind of prize—the Ignoble Prize, I think it's called. In addition to the Ignoble Prize, their colleges got an unexpected benefit—each could now recruit intercollegiate athletes lacking all scholastic aptitude. With the curve in place, coaches could promise prospective "scholar-athletes" they'd make the grade without having to do a lick of academic work. These urban colleges literally pulled themselves up their jock straps. Their colleges turn profits now, and boy, do they ever field great football and basketball teams.

A Sound Financial Footing

Thus, the curve, born out of financial necessity in a few hard-pressed urban colleges, soon spread to colleges and universities throughout the country. Curve-surfing colleges managed to retain virtually all their students. Instead of losing up to two-thirds of their students (and all their tuition payments and parking fines) to academic rigor, universities were able to keep everyone—including the dummies. Even the jocks who can barely read the giant neon sign ("Bountiful Bare Babes") outside the Main Street Men's Club, now hang around campus for years. Sometimes they stay long enough to learn how to read sophisticated books by themselves, like "Green Eggs And Ham." That's what the curve has done. The curve did more than hang on to the jocks. It fattened the coffers of lots of colleges and universities (see Chapter 19). What a great business decision!

So once you enter a university, school officials can count on your payments (tuition, fees, books, services, and parking fines) for at least four years—five or six years if they're lucky and you're not. Unlucky happens when your grades regularly fall near the bottom two percent of the curve.

Every time you totally blow a course by being in the bottom two percent, you need to repeat the course. Then you can stay in college longer and the university gets even more money. The administrators don't mind this at all.

Retention Is In--Curve Is Out

While the curve has transformed college education, there are perceived negative connotations to use of the word curve. Curve is not a sufficiently pedantic term. (Sorry. I have no idea what "pedantic" means, but using my Balderdash approach, "pedantic" seemed to fit in here.) A term like "curve" lacks the flair that academics use to isolate themselves from the masses. No educational funding agency, for example, will look twice at a grant proposal that mentions the term curve. To avoid the curve stigma, administrators invented a new term--one much more pleasing to ears of the pretentious. That term is "student retention." Armed with this new expression, some university administrators have amassed huge sums of money from government and philhellenic (or is that philatelic?) agencies. State U. hasn't learned how to attract "retention dollars." We're still working on it. We'll get it right one day. So out with the curve, in with retention.

With the blessings of these funding agencies, university administrators can keep even the most incompetent student in school as long as the student's money holds out. This makes excellent business sense. You'll love the secure feeling that comes with having a curve firmly in place. It is so much easier this way. Not like it used to be. I really had to struggle when I was a State U. student. I even studied three hours one night. But it is real easy now. No matter what you do or don't do in college, there is always a sheepskin waiting for you. (Oops! I'm not talking about that kind of sheepskin. I'm talking about a diploma.)

So powerful and pervasive is the student retention initiative that most professors have consciously or subconsciously lowered academic standards for their classes by three orders of magnitude (Cliff says that's one thousand times) in the past twenty years (see Figure 11.1). This has really boosted retention. If you don't believe me, look at Table 10.1. Table 10.1 shows the actual answers submitted by State U. freshmen on a basic chemistry exam. Each of these answers was awarded full credit by the professor. I hasten to point out the following facts: (1) the professor presented the questions in essay format (that's much harder than the usual multiple-choice format) and (2) she was teaching only students in the General Major.

A few years ago the State U. president instituted the General Major (GM) specifically for "jock-scholars." The GM is a grab bag of unrelated and undemanding courses. Cliff says the General Major is to college what first semester Pop Tarts is to high school. I don't know what his point is. But then, lots of things Cliff says don't make much sense to me. He says the sole purpose of the GM is to keep "jock-scholars" one nanopoint above a C average. This I get. The head coach makes professors in the GM program dumb down course contents so much that none of the athletes fail. "Too much money is invested in State U. athletes," says the coach, "to have them bust out of college because of some silly chemistry test about noble gasses or royal farts."

That's why some of the "correct" answers in Table 10.1 may seem just a tad off the mark. The General Major is not real strict. Cliff says that very little content is offered in the GM and essentially no performance is expected. I don't know. I looked carefully at the questions in Table 10.1 and they seem pretty tough to me.

TABLE 10.1:
STUDENT RETENTION AS SEEN BY ACCEPTANCE OF THE FOLLOWING ANSWERS ON A CHEMISTRY TEST

Question: What is an atom?
Answer: Atom is the name of the guy who married Eve.

Question: Estimate the number of moles in a liter of water.
Answer: I don't know about water, but my dad says there must be at least 6×10^{23} moles eating up the grass in our back yard.

Question: What is a noble gas?
Answer: A noble gas is a royal fart.

Question: Explain why sodium chloride is able to dissolve in water.
Answer: If it didn't, you couldn't make iced tea appear sweet.

Question: What is a molecule?
Answer: A molecule is the smallest part of matter that cannot be divided evenly by three.

Question: Is it possible to achieve absolute zero?
Answer: Sure! Just take one of these tests.

Question: How many liters are there in a quart?
Answer: I'm not falling for that one! It all depends on what you're weighing.

Question: What is the numerical value of the pH of neutral water?
Answer: I forgot my calculator.

Question: How would you go about finding a square root?
Answer: I'm not exactly sure, but I guess I would start by looking for a square plant.

Question: What is the complete chemical formula for water?
Answer: Well, I know the shorthand formula is H to O. So, I guess the complete formula must be HIJKLMNO. Did I do good?

Hey Doc! Does Speling Count?

    You can see we now have real good systems to keep students from flunking out. We have the curve for all students and the GM for jocks. Because of the GM, even college athletes can now graduate and find jobs. There aren't enough high school physical education positions available for all the graduating jocks, so most of them wind up teaching 10th grade history. History is easy. You just tell the students to memorize lots of dates, like maybe 1492, because it rhymes with ocean blue. Teaching high school chemistry is much too hard.

CHAPTER 11

THE UNIVERSITY PRESIDENTS' STANDARD GRADING CURVE

Facing tight money and projections that ninety-three percent of recruited student athletes would fail, the American Academy of Presidents of Universities (AAPU) went into action. Unfortunately, the AAPU is sometimes confused with the AAUP. They are as different as chalk and cheese. The AAUP, the American Association of University Professors, is a passive, gentile chat group for action-challenged professors. AAUP leaders meet every few days to contemplate, in a cerebral sort of way, what it might be like for a union of professors to defend other members of their profession (other than themselves) or to take some minimal job action. The AAUP regulars really don't like to make waves, so they propagate passive platitudes like "job action."

Job action is a cozy, faculty-club term for what real working people call a strike. (Excuse me! We don't use the word "strike" in the State U. AAUP.) A job action hasn't actually happened at State U. Never even been proposed. Not once in 510 years! But some day, when chapter leaders evolve vertebral columns, the AAUP local may do something. But it's a long, long road from coelenterate to chordate! (Do you know this expression? I haven't a clue what it means, but Cliff likes it.) Several hundred million years of evolution, Cliff says. That's about as long as it takes an AAUP case to get defeated in court. But, despite its evolutionary disadvantage, the local State U. chapter is eons ahead the National AAUP. National is still struggling to emerge from the "primordial soup." If you are waiting for a National AAUP emergence, don't hold your breath—not unless you're an anaerobe.

But I digress. Back in the summer of 1993, the AAPU (the presidents) met in secret to find a common solution to this urgent retention problem. I'm not sure which resort they chose for their secret meeting, but it must have been a plush tropical Caribbean casino of the type they always visit. Their goal was to keep students in school by lowering academic standards. In particular, the AAPU wished to hang onto otherwise academically ineligible athletes.

One Neuron Needed

Up to 1993, university presidents had just two ideas for keeping athletes enrolled. One was the curve for all students. The other was the General Major for "jock-scholars." You already know about the curve and the GM (see Chapter 10). All a "jock-scholar" needs for the GM is one functioning cerebral neuron (Fig. 11.1). Two or three would be much better, but that's asking a lot. When they tested me in college, they found twenty-seven cerebral neurons, so I knew I was in real good shape. With all those extra neurons, I passed out of the GM easy. Cliff says if I can pass out of the GM, it must really be a program for dummies. Cliff's always giving me little compliments. That's why we get along so good. Yet, despite this innovative and imaginative solution to the problem of jock failure, too many 373-pound offensive tackles and 7'8" basketball point-guards were flunking out of college. It was time for a new approach.

UPSGC Secret Unveiled

The AAPU rose to the challenge. The Academy met each summer for the remainder of the decade. They really like that tropical Caribbean casino. Then, on February 22, 1999, the AAPU finally adopted the University Presidents' Standard Grading Curve (UPSGC). Pause here for fanfare, drum roll, and a few pina coladas. This was a groundbreaking accomplishment.

Prior to 1999 every university had its own curve. Some were steep. Some were shallow. Some were flat. So nobody could tell if an A at Podunk State

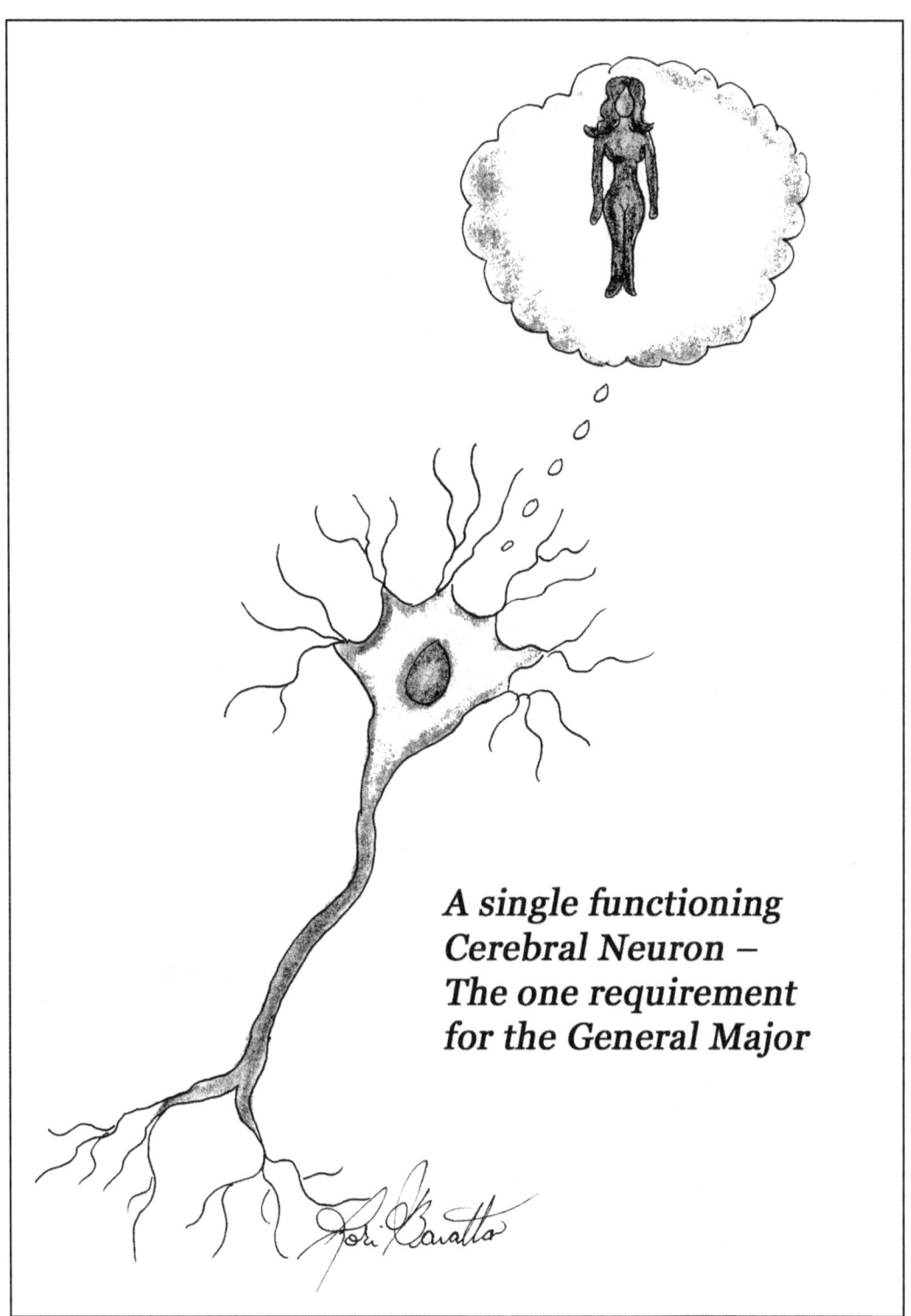

(Fig. 11.1)

College was the same as an A at MIT. The university presidents wanted standardization. With the UPSGC, all grades were placed on the same level — basically A's in most classes.

The UPSGC was meant to remain a secret among university presidents — just like the location of their tropical Caribbean casino hideaway. They planned to administer the UPSGC secretly. But the details of the UPSGC leaked to a student newspaper reporter in Nebraska late that year. Figure 11.2 is likely to be the first published version of the University Presidents' Standard Grading Curve. I probably shouldn't be putting the UPSGC figure in this book. I could get into lots of trouble. But once in a while it feels good to open a can of worms. As a member of the State U. governing board, I suppose I should know what "can of worms" means — something to do with trout fishing, I guess. Anyhow, Figure 11.2 shows the newly adopted UPSGC letter grades superimposed upon accepted standards for university student performance in 1958. We've come a long way.

Degrees Gleefully Guaranteed

The UPSGC took effect just in time for the millennium. Early reports show student retention jumping from sixty-three to ninety-six percent. Even more exciting is the projection that graduation rates for football players may hit double digits. Double-digit retention is a confusing term. It has nothing to do with the number of fingers that survive four years on the gridiron. (That number is usually three.) In this context, the term double digits means at least ten percent of athletes graduate in four years. State U. is working hard to get to double digits. We're at 2.7 percent now. But, hey! That's double digits — a 2 and a 7, right? So what's the big deal? At 2.7 percent we've got to be above the national average.

The UPSGC is wonderful news for high school students considering higher education. It means you can almost be sure you'll get a college degree even if you are a jock. Just be sure your parents keep paying your tuition, fees, and housing, and don't forget to have them pony up for those parking fines. I didn't say this before, but you should know it now. Parking fines can kill you. They'll keep you from graduating. Just when you think everything is a go, you'll get this note from University Parking Services:

Dear Ms. Doe,
According to our records you have an unpaid parking balance of $24,920. Please arrange payment within forty-eight hours. A copy of

this letter is being forwarded to the Office of the Registrar. Failure to pay this outstanding balance will automatically block your graduation. Thank you for your cooperation in this matter.

Take this letter real serious. UPSGC will not get you off the hook with Parking Services. You have to pay. So, with UPSGC, college is just like your parents' home mortgage. So long as your parents deliver a mortgage payment every month, they get to keep the house. So long as you pay all your fees and parking fines, you get to stay in college.

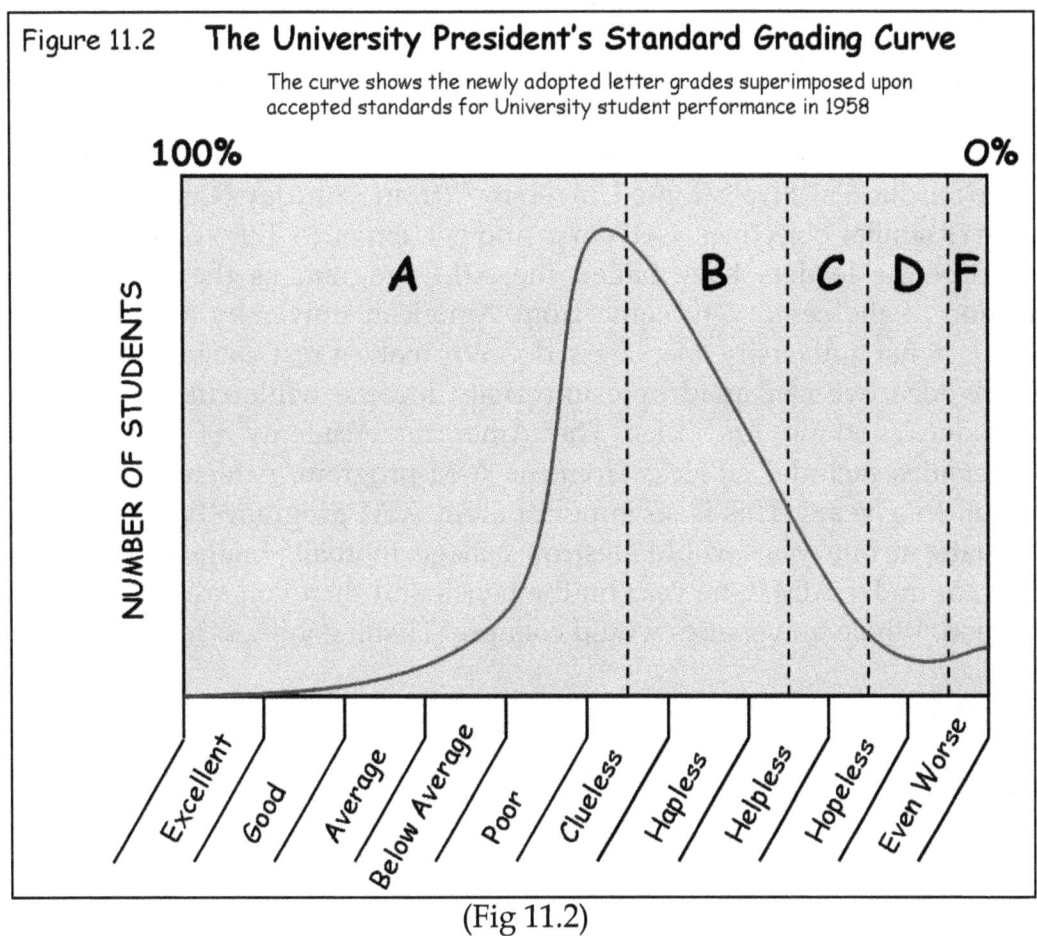

(Fig 11.2)

Accelerated, Intensive Matriculation

As this book was about to go to press, the Nebraska newspaper reporter who blew the whistle on the University Presidents' Standard Grading Curve leaked some new information. It seems that the AAPU is currently considering a novel idea: Accelerated, Intensive Matriculation (AIM). The AIM program will let college students complete their college degrees in just one year. Students in the AIM program will register for the normal fifteen to eighteen credits per semester, but they'll need just thirty-two credits to graduate. However (and this is an important point), AIM program students will have to pay four years' worth of tuition. They will also have to pay four years' worth of fees and housing assessments. Their parking fines will be quadrupled. So the total cost for the AIM program is unchanged from the traditional plan. The big difference is that you cut out three years of courses. This also means you can cut out three years of flipping burgers. You'll be able to start your career—probably in burger flipping—while all your pals under the traditional plan are still sitting in termite-riddled student desks under leaky sewer pipes doing multiple-choice tests in disgusting basement classrooms. AIM is not a bad deal, huh? AIM is a bit less radical than Father Guido Sarducci's "Fiva Minute University" (from Saturday Night Live), but it achieves similar objectives. Get 'em in and get 'em out, Cliff would say.

Corporate leaders have hailed the AIM program as the best business decision of the century to come from American university administrators. This is what university managers do. We make great business decisions. Under AIM, we can quadruple university income while cutting expenses. AIM does nothing for jocks. The American Academy of Presidents of Universities excludes all jocks from the AIM program. Athletes must put in the full four years. This is so important. An AIM program that lets athletes graduate in one year would destroy college football. Imagine a red shirt program under AIM. One year on the bench and then you are out of college for good. Whole universities would collapse. Thank goodness for the AAPU.

Section IV

Your Later College Years

Chapter 12

How to Do Real Good Lab Reports for Your TA

Science Labs

Let's say that you choose to be a science major in college because you want to be a doctor. You'll want to be the MD kind of doctor not the kind your professor is. An MD makes money. A professor just programs computers to teach his or her classes and then gets fired when he is no longer needed (see Chapter 9). As a science major, you'll have dozens of lab reports to write. Lab reports can be a real big pain because you have to put so many words in them. The instructor may want some of the words to make sense. But if you're lucky, your instructor will not be able to read a lick of English, so nothing you write will matter at all.

What's a TA?

TA stands for teaching assistant. You'll need to know about TA's because, for the next four years, TA's will be teaching nearly all of your college courses. They're just inexperienced kids who do all the work the professors should be doing—like teaching. TA's are going to grade your lab reports too. The professor will show up once in a while just to let you know that, at age seventy-nine, he has not yet retired. State U. has no mandatory retirement age for professors, so guys like this seventy-nine-year-old hang around just to build up a huge retirement package. Even though this professor does no teaching, he pretends to be in charge of the class by dropping in from time to time.

Let me tell you more about TA's. TA's are students who have finished college with a BA or BS degree and have returned to college for more abuse. They are also called graduate students. But why would anyone do this? Why would anyone go back to school after spending eight years in grade school, four years in high school, and then four more years in college? I couldn't wait to get out of college myself. Seven years in college was a nightmare for me. So why do TA's stay around even longer? Is it sadomasochism? Is it some kind of death wish, perhaps? Not really. You see, typical students, approaching graduation, have no idea what to do with the rest of their lives. Lucky for me I got a real good job right after college. It was all that football talk at the interview that did the trick for me (see Chapter 16).

You see, a college graduate knows almost nothing about the outside world after years of doing M/C tests. Aside from guessing among the first five letters of the alphabet and flipping burgers, college graduates have no skills. But they know one thing. They know they owe the outside world lots of money. It's a real scary thing to start a working life with a student loan balance of $68,642.98 like I did. But there's a way to avoid paying off your loans. You just stay in school. Student loans can be deferred (that means put off) until you finish all your schooling. That includes graduate school. So lots of students go to graduate school.

Graduate school is the place where TA's go when they come back to college. But graduate school is not really a place—like there's no real graduate school building. Graduate school is just an unfulfilled concept--like the notion of a helpful administrator. Graduate school functions a bit like undergraduate school except that the graduate school courses are a whole lot easier. They only give A's and B's in graduate school. Professors make the courses real easy so students will spend all their time doing research for the professors. This is how professors get rich and famous—by getting graduate students to do their work. No sense making graduate students study for courses if you can get them to do research for free. So lots of college graduates stay in this easy, conceptual school almost forever, to avoid planning for their futures and to avoid paying back $68,642.98. Best of all, the whole time a student stays in graduate school, loan interest does not accrue (that means pile up).

No Skills

Lacking basic skills, the college graduate views the outside world of work and business as a monumental threat. Even that heart-to-heart talk with Momma-san and Papa-san does not ease the fear: "Allight, alleady! Enough with the correge! Do you evel pran to get out? Enough with the tulition payments! Your mothel and I have had it. So kid, if you're not gonna get a leal job, you'll on youl own. No more handouts from us!"[4]

So this is how graduate students become what they are. They start with this heart-to-heart talk where all they do is listen. But what about TA's? What do they do? TA's actually have three full-time jobs. The jobs aren't leal jobs like Momma-san and Papa-san can understand, but they're jobs all the same. TA's take graduate-level classes, they teach undergraduate classes, and they work seventy hours per week for a research professor as a modern indentured servant. Just like college professors, TA's have never received any training to be teachers. They just show up at the assigned time and place and mumble something or other for an hour or so. Often it takes you the whole semester just to figure out what language your TA is mumbling. Knowing what language the TA speaks is not much help. Even in the English department, TA's are not required to speak any English. In Chemistry and Math, they never do.

Pigeons and TA's

If you happen to understand your TA, you may feel he or she has a bad attitude. You are absolutely right. Some TA's have terrible attitudes. But they have reasons. They are greatly overworked and underpaid and they get tired of working in a foreign country. They get no pay for their seventy-hour workweek of research. They just get paid for their teaching. That means their salaries are about sixteen percent of minimum wage. They have enough money for food or lodging, but not enough for both. Most choose food. This is why they have a bad attitude. The park bench is a cold, uncomfortable bed and the pigeons treat them like &%$# (Fig. 12.1).

---

[4] Cliff helped me translate this from Mandarin. I'm not sure he got it all light.

In spite of these feudal working conditions, TA's seem to hang around forever. It beats finding a job and puts off those loan payments. After five or seven or seventeen years (always a prime number, just like with cicadas—Cliff what are cicadas?), the professors in the department get together and decide it's time for the TA to go. The professors have a little ceremony (with cheap, domestic champagne in a screw cap bottle and day-old powdered donuts from the neighborhood convenience store). Then they sign a piece of paper called a PhD. (In chemistry or biochemistry it's called a pH paper.) When a graduate student is presented with a PhD (or a pH paper), he or she is forced to leave. A PhD is like a summons to appear in court, except it's a summons to get out into the real world. Even then, some graduate students won't leave. Instead, they become postdoctoral students and hang around the university for another decade or two trying to get a PPhD (or a PpHpaper). But PPhD's, or post-docs as they are called, get enough salary for both food and rent. They can finally move in off the park benches. The pigeons are pleased to get back their perches—until the next boatload of TA's arrives.

Volunteer to Clean the Attic

Lots of students try to do real good on lab reports. But if you want to go to medical school, you have to do these reports even more better. In fact, you can't make a single mistake--not even on one lab report--or you won't get into med school (see Chapter 14). If you are a pre-med, be sure to let your TA know that you are a pre-med and that you have to get one hundred percent on every report. It is a good idea to write in parentheses right after your name at the top of each report "(PRE-MED)" - just in case the TA forgets. To help you do real good on lab reports, I have listed, in Table 12.1, some important hints that will make your report writing much easier.

William W. Ward

(Fig 12.1)

Hey Doc! Does Speling Count?

TABLE 12.1:
HECTOR'S HELPFUL HINTS FOR DOING REAL GOOD LAB REPORTS

1. Labs are designed for manipulating things (like mutant fruit flies, fresnel lenses, fetal pigs, Florence flasks, frogs and fish, and Freudian slips). They are not designed for thinking. Whatever you do, don't waste a minute of lab time thinking.

2. College lab exercises are just the same as they were in 1971--word for word. So if you have a parent, uncle, aunt, or other aging relative who went to State U., you can find each graded lab report somewhere in that relative's attic. This is a valuable resource, so volunteer to clean the attic. Not only do you get in good with your family for doing a good deed, but you may find all the old lab reports as well. You can sell the ones you don't need to your friends.

3. Even if none of your relatives went to college, you can pledge a fraternity or sorority and have access to all the old lab reports in the house files. Greek societies have an official chapter historian whose job it is to maintain house files filled to the brim with old exams and lab reports. Chapter historian is the most important office in a fraternity or sorority, after president. Without the chapter historian to give everybody old tests and lab reports, the sorority or fraternity could go on academic probation. If grades get real bad, your fraternity or sorority could go on double, secret probation.

    One way fraternities avoid having the whole house on double, secret probation is to pledge a football player. Once the college administration learns that there is a 373-pound offensive lineman in the fraternity, they will leave it alone. Everyone could have a 0.67 grade-point average and nobody would care (0.67 in a 4.0 point system used to be an F in college— now it is probably a low B). Sororities don't have this escape route because the administration doesn't care about women's sports. They have women's sports at State U. because some feminist law says they have to. Anyhow, there just aren't any 373-pound offensive linewomen in college.

4. Be sure to exchange phone and email numbers with your lab partners. This way, sometime after midnight, before the lab report is due (at 8:30

a.m. that morning), you can find out how to do the report from someone in your class who is equally clueless.

5. Do everything in the report by computer. This way, the final report will look real good. The computer will know how to write every sentence real good for you, too, especially if you have purchased a software package like RandGen Post-Millennium Edition (MicroSmooth's most recent random word generator--see Chapter 6). Be sure to tell the computer to put in lots of tables, graphs, and equations. Look around your keyboard. Here you will find three little, tiny keys labeled T, G, and E. These are the keys you push to get tables, graphs, or equations. Push them a lot so you'll get lots of tables, graphs, and equations. All reports in college should have lots of these things. For some subjects, you need statistics. For example, if you have reports in Psychology, Sociology, Meteorology, Ecology, Political Science, Economics, or Planting Wierd Shrubs Over Smelly Old Landfills, you must include lots of statistical tests. This is on account of no data in these fields make any sense without statistics. The idea is to employ so many statistical tests that everyone forgets how meaningless the raw data really are. Computers know how to do this--just push the lowercase S key for statistics. Don't use the uppercase S key if you are looking for statistics. The uppercase S gives you the slope in centipedes per square hour (see Chapter 13).

6. If you find you have to do any work in one of your lab classes, just talk to your professor. The professor is the real old guy who drifts in and out of your lab about once a month. He's just checking to see if the TA ever shows up. Don't confuse the professor with the custodian. The custodian comes by twice a month and does something of value. He empties the trash. When you identify the professor, just tell him that you have already taken twelve lab classes in college (all with grades of A or B) without having to do any work at all. You want to know why this TA requires you to work in class. This is bound to impress.

7. Pick a real smart lab partner who will do all the work and give you all the answers while you wander around the room having fun.

8. If your report is word-for-word the same as your real smart lab partner's, no sweat. You won't get in trouble, even if you get caught. The professor

will do nothing because disputes about cheating are settled by a lesser assistant dean. The lesser assistant dean takes orders from the executive dean. The executive dean's major responsibility (aside from trying to pronounce all 1,726 names of the graduating seniors) is to assign to one of many lesser assistant deans anything that looks like work. The lesser assistant dean will probably want to ignore the cheating incident. He or she also sees work involved.

The executive dean's next most important responsibility is to make real stupid autocratic decisions and then to blame the faculty when these decisions fail. So, if you get turned in for having copied your real smart lab partner's report word-for-word, the dean involved will side with you and against the professor. Deans are jealous of professors because professors have tenure and some deans don't. Lacking tenure means that deans must act as puppets for the central administration. Anything wrong and they get fired. Deans really hate professors who exercise their academic freedom by pointing out the deans' mammoth screw-ups and boondoggles to the rest of the faculty. Deans' jobs are on the line all the time. So a cheating thing is a great opportunity for the dean to get even with professors. So cheat as much as you want. You might as well. After all, you have a senior administration without moral values. Why should you burden yourself with morality when they don't?

9. If your graded lab report comes back covered from one end to the other with words like "gibberish" or "gobbledygook," you are probably doing O.K. Most of the other students' reports are bound to be worse. Even if you get everything wrong, you'll be saved by the University Presidents' Standard Grading Curve (see Chapter 11). With the curve in place, you're bound to get an A, along with most of the other students in the class. This may save your fraternity or sorority's Greek ass. But if you discover that your college has not adopted the University Presidents' Standard Grading Curve, you should apply to transfer to another college or university the next day. Without the curve for protection, there's no telling what kinds of grades they'll give you. They might even give you a C—if so, good-by medical school. Hello Burger Joint.

10. Be sure to put your name at the top of the page.

CHAPTER 13

DOING GRAPHS IN COLLEGE

What Is a Graph?

Lots of courses you take in college (like lab classes, see Chapter 12) will expect you to do graphs. You may not know what a graph is, so let's start with definitions. First off, it's not a "Graf." This is a real good tennis player or a kind of a blimp called a Zeppelin. It's not the other kind of "graf" either. This is something electrical used in physics. Nor is it a tall, spotted African animal that eats leaves from the tops of Acacia trees in Walt Disney's Animal Kingdom. Most of all, it's not a "graft." Graft is doing something illegal for money. That girl I used to see on Friday nights—Cliff said she was doing graft (or was it tricks? I forget). Some politicians and university presidents get all involved in graft. It's not a real good thing to do graft--but they do it anyhow. But I'm getting off track. Just what is a graph?

A graph is a sort of a picture that a computer draws for you if you plug in data or numbers or something like that. It used to be you had to think and do a lot of hard work to make graphs. In those days, you would do tedious mathematical calculations with a slide rule (that's one of those funny Asian things with little beads you slide along parallel rows of wires). Then, hours later, you'd put away the slide rule and draw graphs by hand on something called "graph paper." (If you go to Office Max or Staples to buy graph paper, the seventeen-year-old clerk will give you a very quizzical look and send you on a fifteen-minute-long unguided wild-goose chase to the most remote sections of the store in hopes that you will find "what was that you wanted — graph paper?"). After fourteen more store attendants become involved in the search, someone will recognize once having heard the word "graph paper" and dig out the one remaining pack in the store. It will be polar coordinate graph paper. But now, in the computer age, you don't have to worry about graph paper and you don't have to do any thinking, calculating, or drawing, because computers do the graphs for you (and the pictures are real good, too).

So what about the details? Graphs have things called axes--not the kind for chopping wood or alligator tails (see Chapter 1) and not the kind for axing questions (see Chapter 3). Graph axes have something to do with an X and a Y. If you take biology, you will learn about X and Y, but not the graph-kind of X and Y. The kinds of X's and Y's in biology are all about chromosomes and not about graphs. The kinds of X's and Y's in graphs have something to do with up and down; well, at least one of them does. The other one is about left and right. One of the letters is called the "ordinary" and the other, the "ascension." They should have used A and O instead of X and Y, but that's another story. You don't have to know the fancy names for the X and the Y because the computer will take care of everything for you.

Now you are ready to make a graph. Well, as soon as you have some numbers, that is. When you get the numbers, just plug them into your computer. Use the keys with numbers on them, not the ones with letters. If you get the numbers mixed up, don't worry. The computer will sort everything out and give you a real good picture. After you put all the numbers into your computer, just push the G key (for graph) and then the print key. In a few seconds you'll have a graph ready to turn in to class.

Where To Put the Staple

Making the graph is easy. Now comes the hard part. You will have to decide, completely on your own, which corner of the graph to staple to the rest of your report. This is real hard because your paper is a rectangle. It has four corners. Four choices! That's almost as bad as an M/C test. It's a good thing computer paper is not dodecagonal. You'd never figure out which

Figure 13.1   Locations for the Staple *

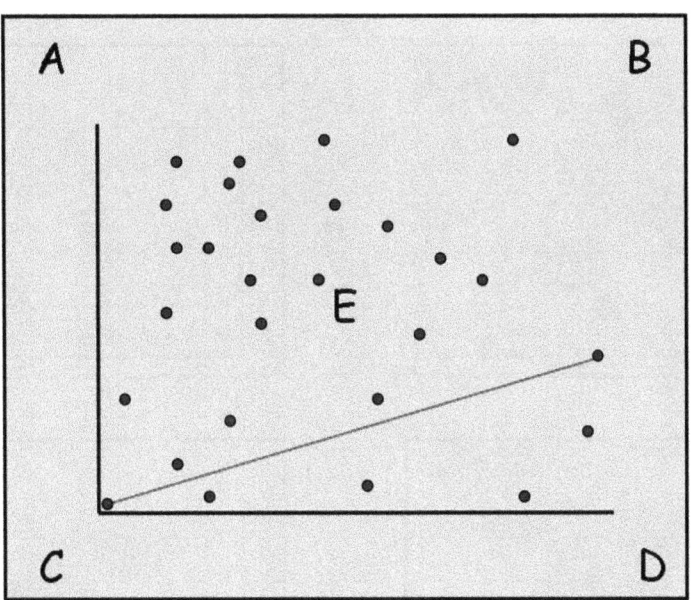

* The staple should be placed in position A,B,C, or D. Don't put the staple in Position E. It might get in the way of a dot.

corner to put the staple on a dodecagon. The computer won't help you here. You're all by yourself on this one. Usually the teaching assistant or professor who grades the lab report won't care how you staple the graph to the report. They're used to reading things from bottom to top. But they can get annoyed when your graph is upside-down and backwards. You'll need to work on this. Refer to Figure 13.1 for suggestions as to where to put the staple.

Connecting the Dots

If you are doing a graph for a science report, you need to know how to tell the computer to draw a straight line. The line must always connect the first dot with the last. If you don't know how to do this, spend some extra time. You may have to work a few hours learning to tell your computer how to connect the first dot with the last dot by a straight line (see Figure 13.2 for

Hey Doc! Does Speling Count?

Figure 13.2   How to Connect the First Dot with the Last Dot Real Good

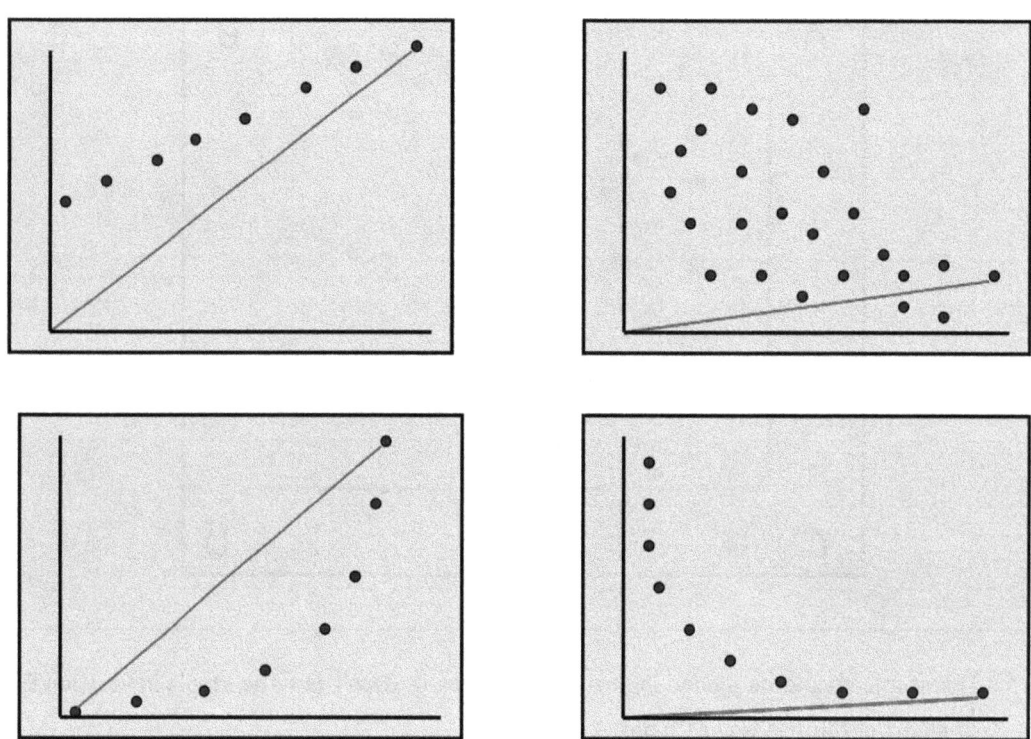

helpful suggestions on how to connect the first dot with the last). Never draw your own line with a ruler. Manual construction may be fast, but this is not a good idea. You should do nothing manually, even if doing so saves time. You need to learn how to depend entirely on the computer. Similarly, don't ever put labels on the graph by hand, even if you cannot get the computer to do this for you. Hand labeling makes the graph look messy. It's much better to turn in a graph that has no axes, no dots, no line, no title, no labels, no page number, no legend, no statistics, and no footnotes than one with a single hand marking. Plus, if you rely on the hand-drawing of dots, lines, and labels, you will never be able to get away with the excuse, when your report is seventeen days late, "Hey, Doc! Sorry it's late and all that. My pencil crashed!"

Sometimes the twelve data points you get for a single experiment don't seem to fall on a straight line. No matter how hard you try, your twelve data points won't line up. Sometimes your computer refuses to draw a straight line between the first dot and the last. This can really be frustrating. When things like this happen, you might be tempted to throw your computer out of your fifth floor window, smashing it to bits onto the concrete pavement below. Never do this during class-change period when the sidewalk is loaded with students. A passer-by might look up, see the computer hurtling down toward the ground like a speeding bullet, and then gently catch it in his or her arms. If this happens, you will have to walk down five flights of stairs, retrieve the computer, walk back up the five flights, and try all over again.

A better choice than smashing your computer onto the pavement might be to simplify your graphing program. Instead of squeezing all twelve data points onto the same graph and confusing your computer, tell it to draw twelve separate graphs, each with one data dot. Well, it's really two dots if you count the origin—that's where the ordinary and the ascension come together to make their own dot. With the origin and just one extra data dot per graph, it will be real easy for your computer to draw straight lines. Even if no passer-by saved your computer, even if it smashed to bits on the pavement, your computer probably will remember how to draw twelve separate straight lines, so long as each has just one data point (plus the origin).

Not only will a smashed computer be able to perform this simple function, but your professor will congratulate you for your ingenuity. If you can turn in a report with twelve graphs instead of one, you will get a lot more credit. Figure 13.3 shows how your graph would look if you tried to crowd all twelve data points onto the same graph. Figure 13.4 shows how things would look if you made twelve separate graphs, each with one data point. As you compare Figure 13.3 with Figure 13.4, you are sure to notice how impressive twelve separate graphs can be.

Centipedes Per Square Hour

Learning to connect the first dot to the last dot is real important. The first dot (the origin, remember) is where the ordinary and the ascension come together and the last dot is, well, the last dot. All the other dots are just there to make the graph look important. Graphs with one data dot are easy. Things get complicated when you have two data dots (in addition to the origin). Your computer will have to struggle a bit if there are two data dots. After your computer has drawn a graph, just push the uppercase S key and you'll get the slope in units of centipedes per square hour. Don't use the lowercase S

Figure 13.3   When Your Computer Fails to Connect the First Dot with the Last Dot

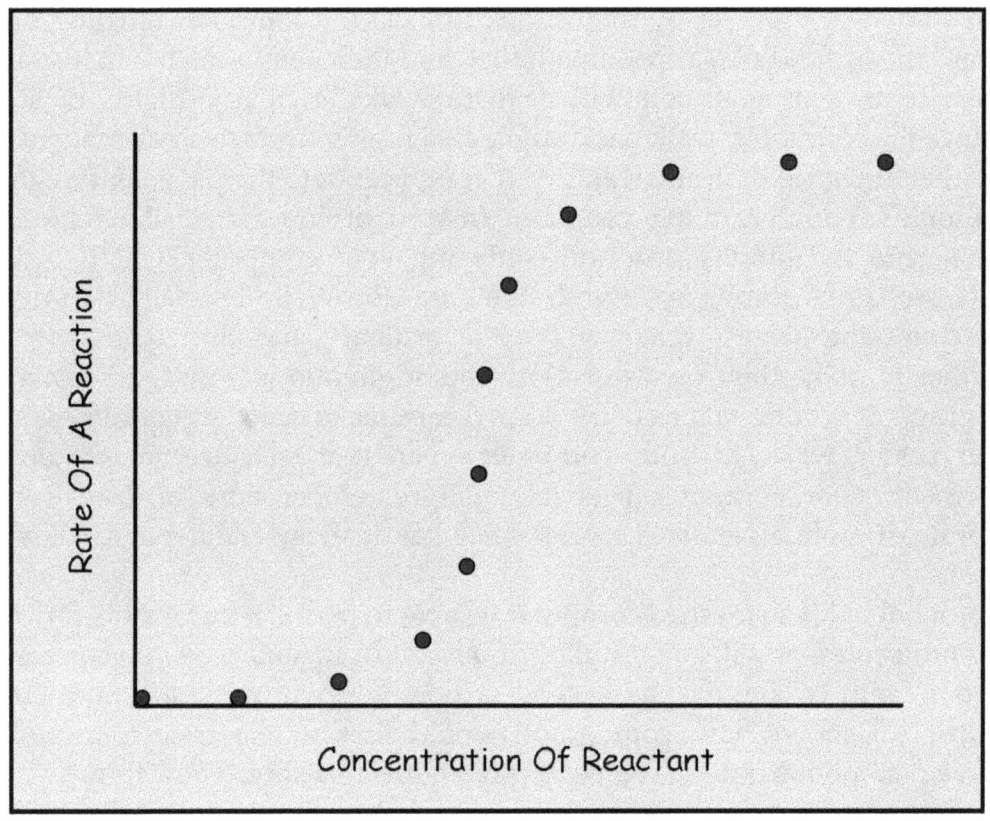

key yet. That will get you a whole bunch of statistics. Save that key for later. Now, about units. Units are like fractions with an enumerator on top and a denunciator on the bottom. But units are a bit different from fractions. Fractions use numbers. Units use words instead of numbers. Units are real important. All graphs should have units.

Some units are more popular than others, like centipedes per square hour. Always select popular units. A few other good ones to use are minutes per square mole, liters per femtofathom, and zirconium cubed per ring. Cubic minutes and molecules absorbed per photon are some other popular units. The important thing here is to choose units that sound impressive and erotic (or is that exotic? I think erotic is right). Professors are deeply moved by erotic

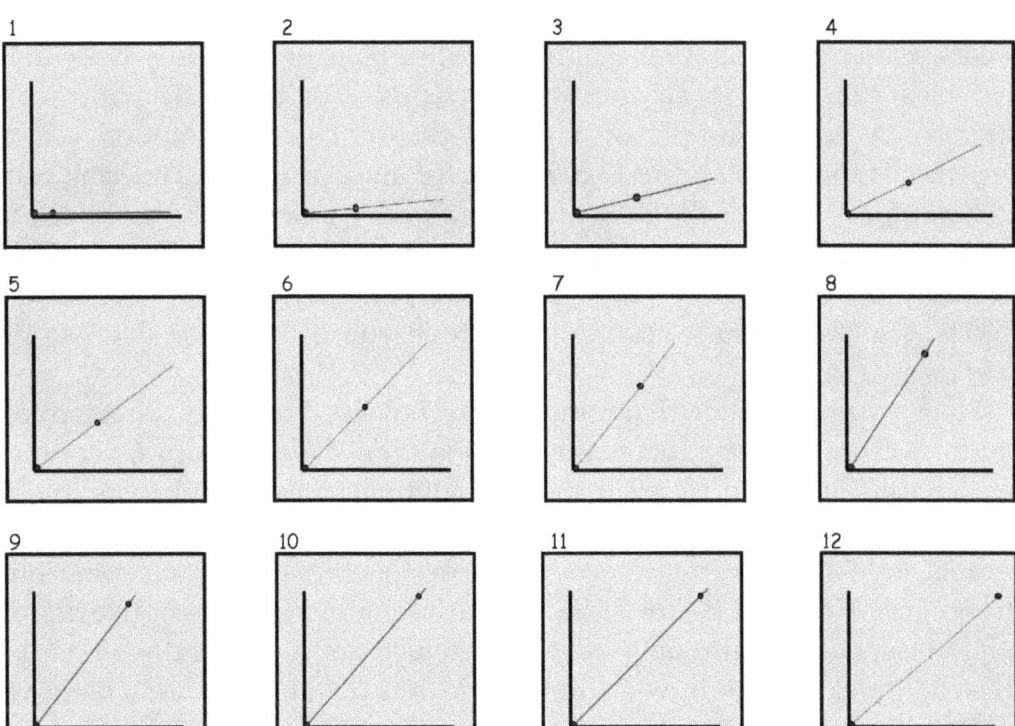

Figure 13.4 Twelve Separate Graphs, Each with One Data Point - Even a Smashed Computer Can Do This

and impressive sounding units and will give you real good grades as a result.

Planting Wierd Shrubs Over Smelly Old Landfills

Sometimes the computer will have a "follow-the-dots" program built into it. This is good for those activity books you used on rainy days when you were three years old and walking around in droopy training pants. Such books have a bunch of numbers you connect, in proper numerical order, to trace out a cuddly teddy bear or a fluffy bunny rabbit or something just as loveable—like a furry tarantula. Follow-the-dots graphing routines are not too good in college science courses (that's Biology, Chemistry, Physics, Biochemistry, etc., in case you've forgotten). Science professors are not crazy about teddy-bear graphs. But follow-the-dots programs might be fine for subjects like Psychology, Sociology, Meteorology, Political Science, Ecology, Economics, or Planting Wierd Shrubs Over Smelly Old Landfills.

In these non-science fields, graphs often look like a close-up of the Milky Way Galaxy. The dots are spread out like tiny stars all over the page. This is called a scatter plot or scatter diagram. Scatter plots are basically useless, but what else can you do in non-science fields. You're stuck with scatter diagrams. A good example of a scatter diagram, with profound celestial overtones, is shown in Figure 13.5. Except for an occasional wandering comet or asteroid, the stars of the Milky Way are pretty much in the same relative positions from day to day. A graphic presentation of the Milky Way looks like a scatter plot, but a Milky Way plot means something. In lots of academic subjects, scatter diagrams change every time you collect new data, so they never mean a thing.

When you get scatter diagrams in Psychology, Sociology, Meteorology, Political Science, Ecology, Economics, or Planting Wierd Shrubs Over Smelly Old Landfills, it's hard to tell if there is anything meaningful there and it's hard to tell where to draw the line. You shouldn't let the computer connect the dots unless you want to see Orion or the Big Dipper or some other astronomical sign (see figure 13.5). Similarly, you can't connect the first dot with the last dot, because nobody can tell which dot is first and which is last. If the computer tries to draw a straight line, it is not always sure whether the line should slope up from the left or slope down from the right. So scatter diagrams take a little extra computer time. Be patient. You have to learn to trust your computer.

When your computer is done making a graph, you know that it has picked the right line because of all the statistical tests it will print out when you push the lower case S key. The results of the statistical tests will be printed just to the right of the graph, as they are in Figure 13.6. Be sure to include in your report lots of long and complicated statistical test results. Good choices are linear least-squared transgressions, efficients of variation, standard mean of the error, Boston-T analysis, variations on the occipital condyle, route mean square route analysis, and mean angle of the dangle. Use a whole bunch of statistical tests. You don't have to know what these tests mean, because your computer does (and chances are your professor doesn't). You just have to know that such tests are impressive and erotic, especially the ones generating at least nine numbers like 0.684622775. The zero, by the way, doesn't count when it is on the left. (Nobody ever told me why some zeros count and others don't. I guess people learn this in high-level math classes like G-string theory — see Chapter 3.)

College professors in fields with scatter diagrams will want to see lots of statistical tests. They also like lots of real long numbers, like 0.684622775, because long numbers show them you like their subjects real good. If you can't get real big numbers, your computer must be too old. Time to hit Mom and Dad up for a new one. They'll be delighted to learn that you're upgrading (that means replacing) your nearly new computer in order to get better looking graphs with nine-digit numerical printouts of route mean square routes. Your mom and dad will gladly fork over $1999.49 for the most powerful PC you can find. As soon as you get your new computer, be sure to study Figures 13.1 through 13.6. You need to know how to do outstanding graphs like these right away, before your brand new, expensive computer becomes obsolete.

Figure 13.5   A Typical Milky Way-Type Graph*

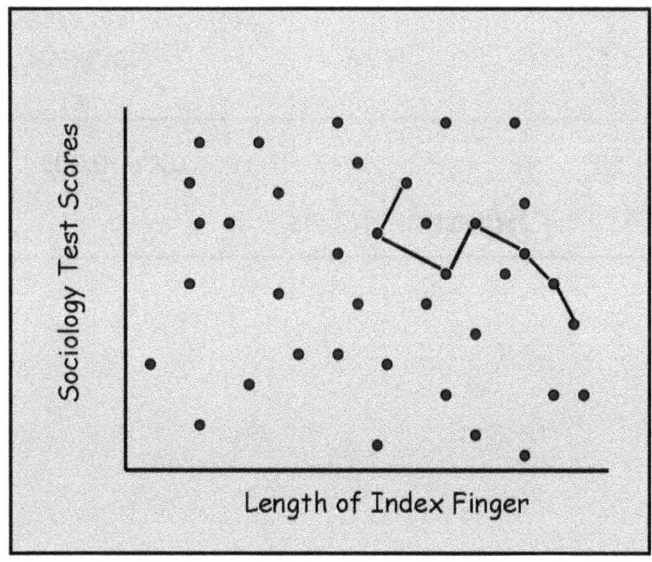

*This sort of graph is not too good for science courses, but it is fine for courses in Psychology, Sociology, Meteorology, Political Science, Ecology, Economics, or Planting Wierd Shrubs Over Smelly Old Landfills. The lone dot in the dipper is statistically significant, based on the root mean square Variance of Konningsberg's "Polaris Algorithm".

Figure 13.6   A Fine Job at Graphing as Demonstrated by all the Great Statistics

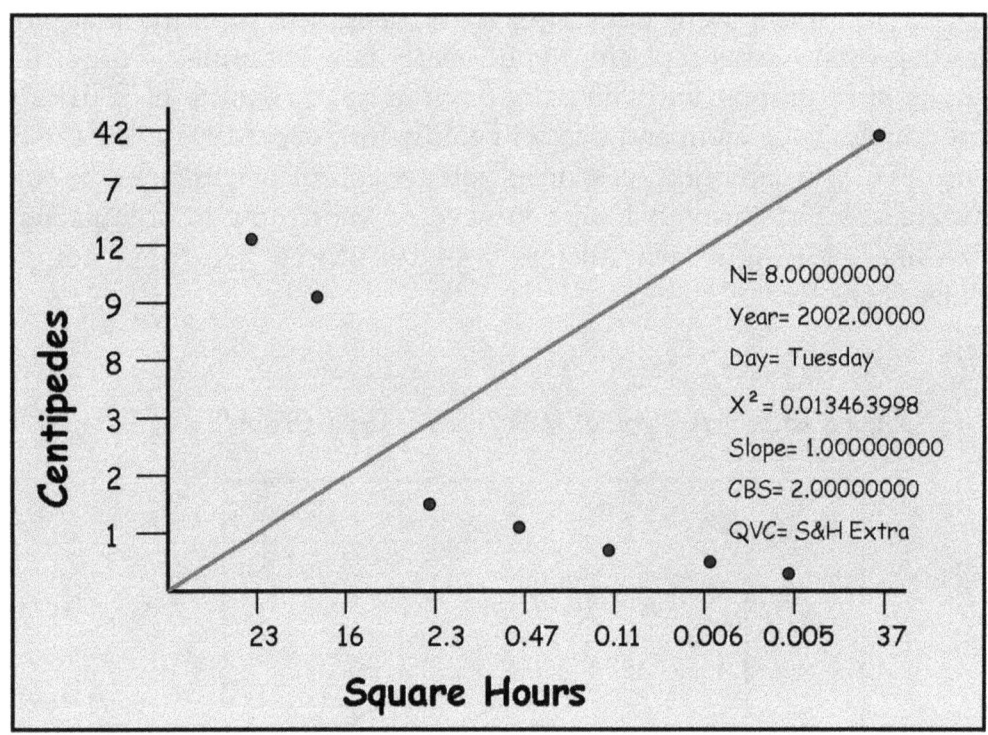

CHAPTER 14

HECTOR'S ADVICE FOR PRE-MED STUDENTS

Pre-meds are college students who expect to go to medical school when they graduate. Now, this is a big group. About ninety-seven percent of college freshmen are pre-meds. The rest of the freshmen are football or basketball players. Pre-meds are different from all other college students because, unlike football and basketball players, they must make A's on every test and every quiz. They have to average 4.00000000 (straight A's--to nine significant figures) for eight semesters in order to get into medical school. Medical schools just want students who make all A's. Unless students get all A's, there is no chance for them to get through a demanding medical school curriculum. Medical students have to be able to memorize about 157,622 human body parts—like the humorous (see Chapter 6).

Learning bones like the humorous is easy (it's the funny bone). But memorizing the name of each individual capillary in the circulatory system and each individual alveolus in the lung, now that's real tough, especially when you can't make one mistake. Make one mistake when you finally have your own medical practice (mess up the name of a single alveolus, for example) and you're dead meat for some aggressive medical malpractice lawyer.

Pre-meds don't need to think or solve problems. They just need to memorize everything (like the names of fifty-seven reproductive parts of twelve species of sub-tropical angiosperms) and get all A's. If you don't get all A's as a pre-med you're out of luck. Even saying "Good Morning" to a C+ student can lower your grade from 4.00000000 to 3.99999999. That's why pre-meds only associate with other pre-meds. They can't afford grade deflation by association. You see, an average of just 3.99999999 is simply not good enough to get into medical school. Back when I was a student, 3.99999999 was a great pre-med average. Not any more. So if you're a pre-med and you get one-tenth of one point wrong on a 100-point trial quiz in the first week of your freshman year, you should immediately make appointments to see each of your instructors. (Brush up on your erotic Eastern languages, first.)

Everything a Pre-Med Does Has To Be Right

As a pre-med, you should begin each appointment by stating firmly and convincingly, "I am a pre-med so I have to get everything right in college. I cannot afford to lose that 1/10th point on a 100-point trial quiz." Be sure to beg and plead by saying, "Please, please! If I don't get credit for that 1/10th point on your 100-point trial quiz, it will keep me out of medical school. You have to raise my grade."

Just talk about grades. Never talk about course content or about the reasons why you may have lost one-tenth of one point out of 100. Just indicate over and over that you are a pre-med so you have to get everything right. This sort of approach always leaves a positive impression on your professor. Few professors can resist raising your grade when you reveal you're a pre-med and when you beg for more points because you must get everything right.

I can tell you what else carries a lot of weight. Saying you came to every class, took every test, nodded respectfully with each failed attempt at humor by the professor, and sat every time in the same seat (#537) from which you asked lots of excellent, provocative, thoughtful questions (see Chapter 7). That's what carries a ton of weight. Try every trick you can think of. Something is bound to work.

The most successful pre-med I ever met was able to raise his four-year cumulative grade point average from 1.63 to the mandatory 4.00000000 just by being good at begging and pleading. Twelve U.S. medical schools accepted him and he had a difficult time deciding which offer to accept. As a practicing surgeon, he's had some hard luck recently. Cliff said he's in jail for medical malapropism or something like that. He hired a State U. lawyer to handle his case. No wonder he's in the slammer. State U. lawyers can't do anything right. They're so bad no private law firm would hire them. They have only three employment options—work for the military, work for a university, or sell pencils along with the bag people on street corners.

Military standards of legal competence are just too high and professional pencil salesmen and bag people refuse to be seen with lawyers. Bag people shove these lawyers off their city street corners so as not to be embarrassed by association. That leaves universities as the employment option of last resort. We have more than our share of "last resorts" at State U. That's for sure.

You didn't buy this book to hear about university lawyers and bag people. Let's get back to pre-meds. The one I remember best was this real hot co-ed who liked me to hang out with her on long summer nights. She earned a four-year average of 3.99896632 in her pre-med curriculum. But she was not very skilled at begging and pleading (about academic matters, that is) and so finished college with a 3.99896632 final average. As this average is not nearly high enough for acceptance to an American medical school, she wound up at the Galapagos Podiatry College and Ecological Preserve. She now practices medicine in the State U. health center, using her training in podiatry to diagnose foot-related, sexually transmitted diseases (see Chapter 5).

I Bet You Look Hot In White

If a professor knows you're a pre-med and still refuses to hike your grade, you should make an appointment to see your university president or a member of the university's Governing Board. If you're a real hot co-ed, come see me. Steer clear of Cliff. He has a reputation. Neither the college president nor any of us on the State U. Governing Board knows anything about pre-med curricula (or any other curriculum). We don't want to know anything either. We're too busy trying to pay for three complete football coaching staffs. We've got the current staff on seven-year contracts, the former staff on five-year contracts (fired last year), and an earlier staff on seven-year contracts (fired three years ago). These sports matters are very important worries. We have no time for educational matters in our busy schedules. We'll want to get rid of you on the spot. (Well, there are exceptions for real hot co-eds, if you get my drift.) The best way for us to get you out of our hair

Hey Doc! Does Speling Count?

is to change your grade--no questions asked. However, this speedy grade change will come about only if you are clever enough to begin your conversation with a complementary statement. One that works is, "Wow! The football team seems to be doing great under the new coaching staff, despite its 0 and 9 losing record."

Another good opening line is, "Damn, you're good looking for an older guy." (Fig. 14.1) (But let's not go there.) Whatever you do, make no reference to the university's having four fired head coaches and thirty-nine fired assistant coaches under contract for the next several years with severance packages totaling $7.8 million. This is just not good politics. Good luck in medical school. I bet you look hot in white!

(Fig. 14.1)

CHAPTER 15

THE EFFORTLESS HONORS PROJECT

If you do real good in your first three years of college, you may be encouraged to do a senior honors project. You probably don't know what senior honors projects are all about. Let me tell you. They are research projects you do in your senior year under the direction of a professor. The idea seems great, especially if you are obsessed with padding your college resume. But don't be fooled. It's not necessarily a good deal. The professors just want you to do their research for free.

Here's how it works. In the spring of your junior year, if you're a real good student, professors will surround you like a swarm of mating dragonflies sniffing erotic pheromones. This swarming is just the beginning of the professors' springtime honors-recruiting frenzy. Soon the successful professor will roll out the red carpet as he escorts you through his multimillion-dollar laboratory. He'll dangle in front of you the promise of fame, fortune, and several Nobel Prizes—all before you finish your first college degree. That's the usual line. But if you're a real hot co-ed, he'll suggest long, intimate "scientific discussions" in his private office. You'll understand the meaning of long, intimate "scientific discussions" as soon as he locks the office door behind you.

You may feel flattered with so much attention, but you're really getting set up for exploitation (if you know what I mean). The professor is recruiting you to perform for free. Be wary, especially if you see a well-worn set of kneepads hanging on the wall. Before you launch into a time-consuming and tedious undergraduate honors research project that earns you no money, ties up your Friday nights, and is bound to fail, stop! Stop and look around. Don't plunge into anything without thinking first about values and goals. Not just the professor's goals, either. Pay careful attention to the values and goals your university's senior administrators hold dear.

Back Lot Façade

Let me digress a bit more. I want to tell you about the State U. senior administrators and those other Board members. They're all energetic and ambitious men and women. They work real hard. They work hard to feather their own nests, that is. They see the university primarily as a tool for their own personal growth and self-aggrandizement. (That's the biggest word I know, so I just stuck it in here.) They act like big shots. It's such a pain for me and Cliff having these jokers around all the time. They make dumb decisions involving hundreds of people and millions of dollars. They hang around with others who do the same things. This makes them feel important. Do they care about you? Are you kidding? Do they care about the other students and faculty? Not a chance. Do they care about the university in general? Well, that's a tougher question. It would seem so because they talk every day about making the university a better place. But is this their true goal? I think not. I think that what matters to most State U. administrators is the appearance of a fine university, not the substance. Big, fancy administration buildings are a huge part of the "Back Lot Façade" (Fig. 15.1). In creating a positive appearance for the university, substance may be drawn in. And that's O.K. Administrators are not looking for substance, but they won't oppose it either.

To the president, State U. is like a Hollywood movie set. What matters to him is the illusion produced by the façades on the back lot. One wall on each building is all the set needs. Of course, it should be the front wall. Having four walls per building with something inside the building doesn't add anything to the overall movie. The movie viewer sees only the façade. The other walls and the insides of the buildings don't count at all.

State U. is just like a phony movie set. Students, faculty, and staff know

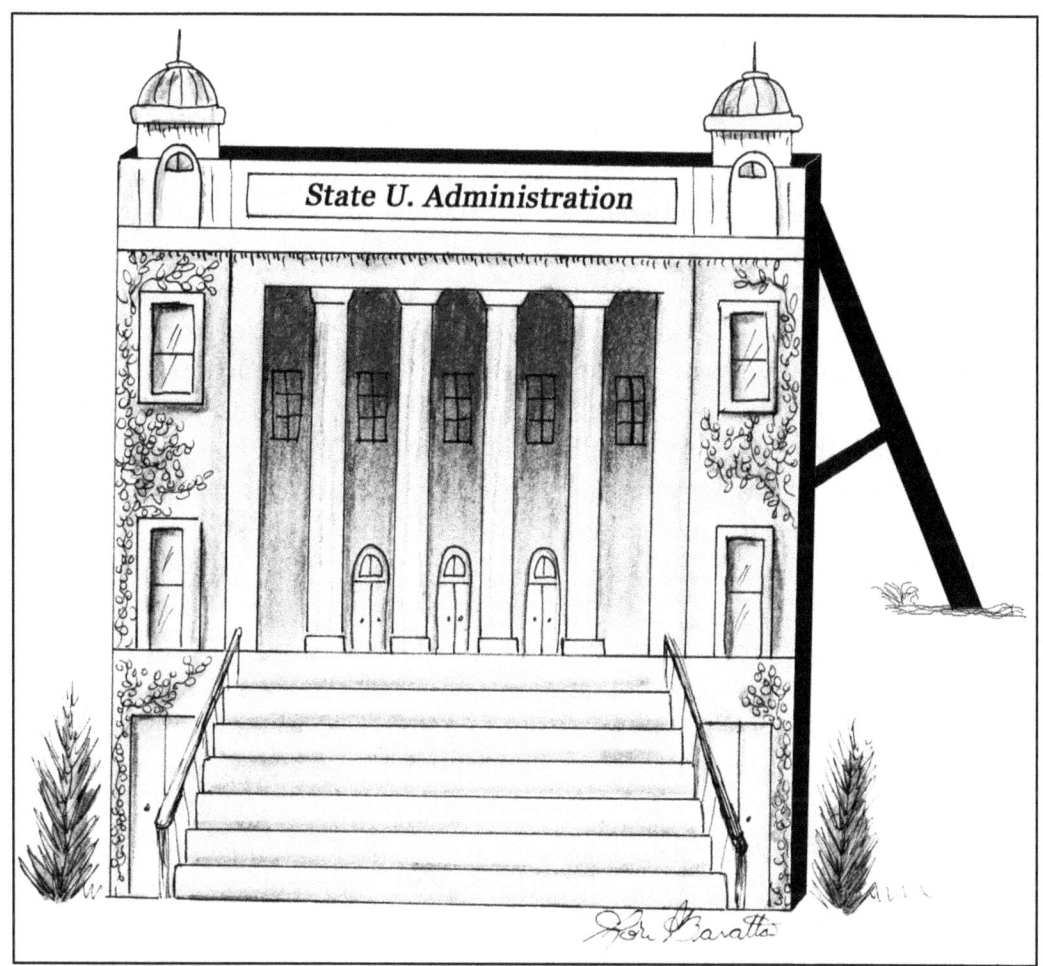

(Fig. 15.1)

this, but the State U. president doesn't care. The viewers of his movie are people who never look beyond the façade. His audience includes state legislators on the lookout for free NFL tickets and a good political image, self-serving corporate leaders trying to convince him to fund silly research centers like the Cancer Cure Candy Center, wealthy alumni hoping to be recognized with campus street names, journalists trying to curry favor by reporting precisely what the State U. PR team ships out to the state's newspapers with hourly press releases, and sports fans who come to all the State U. football games. Well, we need the football fans, but I wish they would make bigger cash donations so we can start winning games for a change. That's the president's audience—the whole motley crew. Most of the people on the

Governing Board are no better. For them and for the president, a façade is all that's needed. Me and Cliff, we're different.

A Few Fools Might

The university's image or national reputation (its façade) comes largely from male gossip and chitchat in bars, brothels, bodegas, and barbershops. Where else would men talk—certainly not in the men's fashion section of Wal-Mart? Shopping for clothes takes men about twelve seconds a year. "Yep! That's my size. I'll take two dozen." When men do stop for lengthy conversations, it's always in bars, brothels, bodegas, and barbershops. What's the topic of conversation—college football, naturally. I go to the Main Street Men's Club all the time, so I hear what everyone is saying about State U. football. But they're always complaining. Instead of complaining, they should be making donations to the Bulldogs Boosters Club. Here's what I heard last Saturday night:

> "What the hell is wrong with the State U. athletic director? Can't he get a better coach? With all the money I'm forking over for my kid's college tuition, at least State U. should be able to find a decent coach—one who knows how to recruit. All the top prospects go out of state. Who's that guy we lost last week? Fendermacher or something like that. They say he's well over 425 lbs. But we lost him just like we lose most of the all-state players. How can State U. compete in Division 1A when we can't recruit a single offensive lineman over 400 pounds? It's high time we got some real horses up front."

So this is how State U. gets its image. And it's not a real good image, that's for sure. The State U. president's posturing and PR efforts could help build a better image, if anybody believed what he had to say. A few fools might—like those other people on the Board. Me and Cliff just think the president is a buffoon. The fact of the matter is that State U. has a crummy administration, a demoralized faculty, a lack-luster student body, a starving educational system, and a crumbling research infrastructure. Yet, if we could just turn our football program around, we could get back on top. Then all that football and basketball brothel babble would work to our advantage instead of cutting us down. If we don't start investing big bucks in the State U. sports program, there's no way the university will get a decent national reputation.

What's His Name? Pablo? Pluto? Plato?

So how could this little diatribe (another "Cliff Note") possible relate to student honors research projects? Simple! Research projects are typically all substance and no façade—the antithesis (Cliff again) of a university administration that is all façade and no substance. Research projects are meant to be rich in substance. Sometimes career researchers spend decades building substance with no hint of façade. Researchers build so little façade that they can't explain to the general public what they do. Sometimes they have trouble answering innocent questions like "What's to come of all this research? How many years are you going to study those silly albino tomatoes of yours?" And, "Don't you have a cure for cancer yet?" Or, "You mean, after twenty-five years, you're still reading one guy's old books? What's his name? Pablo? Pluto? Plato? Won't you ever be done?"

This is the lay public speaking. They'll pretend otherwise, but senior college administrators are no more sophisticated. So why concentrate on the substance of your honors research project? This may be plain foolish. The State U. system only recognizes and rewards the superficial. Make your honors project as superficial as everything the administration does.

Focus On Superficiality

So take a lesson from your university's president and other senior administrators. Don't spin your wheels building substance when nothing counts in their world but appearance. Go with the flow. Follow their leads. Make life easy for yourself. Create an entirely superficial honors research project. All façade. My suggestions are in Table 15.1.

TABLE 15.1:
CREATING A TRULY SUPERFICIAL HONORS RESEARCH PROJECT — THE HECTOR METHOD

1. Find an impressive-sounding project requiring almost no effort on your part. Let the title of your project be its façade. Build it up. Puff it out. Use lots of fancy words. Embellish! Embellish! Embellish! Make your project title an impressive, but entirely superficial, piece of work. But don't spend much time. If you are working for six academic credits, do the whole thing in about thirty minutes. If you are working for twelve academic credits, you might spend an hour. For suggestions as to titles, see Tables 15.2 through 15.4.

2. Choose only upper-level administrators to serve as directors of your research project. It has been ages since top administrators did anything useful at the university. I know. I observe them. They may welcome the opportunity to supervise your research. But, rest assured, they will have no interest in any project of yours. In fact, they will be fearful of revealing their profound ignorance of everything scholarly. So they won't read a word of your honors thesis. It will remain unopened. Their only contribution will be to say, upon returning your honors thesis, "Looks nice! Uh. Where do I sign?" So long as your thesis title is impressive, you could glue your title page right onto the cover of your unused Webster book and turn it in as an honors thesis. Administrators will not want to expose their ignorance by opening the book. It's true. It has always been true. Remember what you learned in second grade? The emperor has no clothes. College emperors have no clothes either. They're also short on skills and morals.

3. But be sure the top-rank administrator chairing your honors research committee has no interest in the subject you've chosen. Otherwise, he or she may try to read past the title page. This could be trouble. If your administrator/thesis chair sees the word "aardvark" followed by a whole string of other A-words and then B-words and so forth all the way to Z-words and finally ending with "Zyrian", he or she could grow suspicious. Perhaps the chairperson will think you cheated. Perhaps the thesis is not your own work. Perhaps you had help from a student named "Webster." A clever administrator might go so far as to ask the registrar if there's a student by the name of "Webster" in your graduating class. While this probably won't happen, it's a good idea for you to check out the names of the graduating seniors, yourself. If there happens to be a "Webster," quick, get a photograph of your administrator/chairperson in a compromising situation. You might need to extort a favor. He or she would do the same, you may be sure, if the roles were reversed.

Now here are some Hector-approved titles for honors-thesis projects. I made them all up by myself. I think they're great. Don't you? Let's say that your honors project is in the field of life sciences. Suppose it's in protozoan biology. Don't even think of picking a title like "The Biology of the Amoeba." A title like this oozes with substance, but it lacks all elements of a good façade. That makes it a bad choice. Refer to Table 15.2 for a good alternative title.

TABLE 15.2:
HECTOR'S REAL GOOD TITLE FOR AN AMOEBA PROJECT

> "A CRITICAL AND COMPARATIVE EVALUATION OF THE RATES OF PSEUDOPODIAL RETRACTIONS IN RESPONSE TO NEGATIVE STIMULI OF TWO POPULATIONS OF THE THECATE AMOEBA BLOBULOUS OBSCURUS IN ISOLATED PUDDLES OF RAINWATER NEAR THE SOUTHERN SHORE OF LAKE MENDOTA WISCONSIN DURING THE SPRING OF 1999."

Now you're cooking! Nobody is going to want to read past this title, certainly not an important university administrator. So paste the title right onto your Webster book and you've got twelve credits for an hour's work. Good going!

What if your subject is early American folklore? As a thesis title, "Early American Folklore" sucks. It has no façade. Someone might just decide to read it. You should choose a much more impressive sounding title like the one in Table 15.3.

TABLE 15.3:
HECTOR'S REAL GOOD TITLE FOR A FOLKLORE PROJECT

> "A COMPREHENSIVE REVIEW OF THE COLLECTED ESSAYS AND MONOGRAPHS OF JOHNNY APPLESEED FROM 1783 TO 1784 AND THE IMPACT OF THESE WRITINGS ON THE DEVELOPMENT AND MATURATION OF PRECOLUMBIAN BALSA WOOD SCULPTURE BY INFLUENTIAL SHAMANS IN A REMOTE VILLAGE OF PERUVIAN INDIANS LIVING AT THE EDGE OF THE TREE LINE ON THE WESTERN SIDE OF THE ANDES MOUNTAINS."

Now that's an impressive title if I say so myself. If this title doesn't turn off potential readers, I don't know what would. Go for it!

Finally, if your field is cancer biotechnology, you must be very careful. Cancer biotechnology has broad general interest, even among administrators. An administrator might find a title like "A New Cure for Cancer" sufficiently gripping to read on. You can't afford to let this happen. So, in this field, you need a powerful strategy to make your title a major turn off. Table 15.4 offers a much better example—one with a huge, impressive façade.

TABLE 15.4:
HECTOR'S REAL GOOD CANCER TITLE

> "EVALUATION OF THE TUMOR REDUCTION POTENTIAL OF A RACEMIC MIXTURE OF BIPHENYLDIHALODIMETHYLTRIHYDROXYAMINE COMPOUNDS GENERATED BY SOLID STATE COMBINATORIAL CHEMISTRIES ON PROPRIETARILY ACTIVATED SUBNANOMETER DIAMETER SUPERFICIALLY POROUS SILICA GEL PARTICLE SURFACES AND ANALYZED IN CHINESE HAMSTER OVARY CELLS BY PHASE MODULATED FLUORESCENCE ANISOTROPIC MODIFICATIONS OF AN OTHERWISE STANDARD FLUORESCENCE ACTIVATED CELL SORTER."

So get out the Webster book and the glue stick. This title is a real winner. Total façade and not an ounce of substance. Is it worth twelve credits? At least!

Chapter 16

Choosing a Major

College First, Major Later

By now you have already spent lots of time at a real good college--based, of course, on its football reputation, stylish school colors, macho team symbol, and convenient 300-mile distance from Mom and Pop (see Chapter 1). So, as you approach graduation, you must finally ask the question all students avoid like the plague, "Does the college I have been attending all these years teach any of the courses I need to graduate with a degree in Ornamental Aquaculture?"

It may seem backwards picking your college at age fourteen, spending your older teenage years drifting aimlessly through easy college courses like Mammiferous Anatomy or Ancient Greek Cuisine because they fit into your fast-food-restaurant work schedule, and then, a month before graduation, considering the required classes for a major. Don't sweat the small stuff. Most students spend hours and hours worrying about their major only to change their minds sixteen times before graduation. This is no big deal. In fact, you can get away with changing majors right up until the graduation handshake from your dean.

Graduation day will be the first time you've laid eyes on the dean. He's no matinee idol, by the way. Even if he's never seen you before, he won't care about your switching majors. He is far too busy trying to learn how to pronounce 1,726 wierd student names. Last year the State U. Arts and Sciences dean mispronounced 287 names at graduation and got into big trouble with the Governing Board. The Board chairman was livid. "I'm not paying the salary of a college dean who can't pronounce the name of my niece," he screamed across the boardroom.

Correctly pronouncing the names of 1,726 graduating seniors he has never seen, let alone met, is the dean's biggest administrative responsibility. That's why he gets such a huge salary. His job is on the line if he screws up again. The dean is very nervous. He's already having big trouble with Zybylbd Bvlspzk. And there are worse names at the end of the alphabetical list.

Preoccupied with pronunciation, the dean will have no clue you just changed majors that morning. If you decide you don't like pharmacy, just switch to phrenology. It is easy to switch from pharmacy to phrenology, from psychology to physics, or from physical education to philosophy on graduation day because all these majors begin with the letter P. Such changes won't mess up the registrar's computer-alphabetized list of majors. Just don't try switching from astronomy to zoology at the last minute. It won't work. The first letters (A and Z) are much too far apart in the alphabet for the registrar to handle.

Bulldogs in the Branch

Choice of majors is not important because your future employer will not ask much about your college education. Employers (male or female) are interested in your cooperative manner, pleasant disposition, corporate loyalty, mature work ethic, enthusiastic team spirit, and your ability to generate lots of trashable one-line memos. Try not to get a female interviewer. With a woman behind the desk, there's no predicting where the conversation will go. You have no way to prepare. She'll come up with the craziest subjects and she'll want you to do all the talking. What kind of an interview is that? When you spot a female interviewer, you might try the "Oops, I must be in the wrong room" routine. Usually this fails and she makes you come in for the interview. Now you're in big trouble.

Let's say you're applying for a job as a plutonium regeneration engineer in a neucular power plant. After exchanging pleasantries that go on forever, the female interviewer will probably break the ice by asking you to evaluate Richard Burton's performance in the Broadway opening of "Camelot." If this happens, just tell her how good Burton was in the second act when he sang "On the street where you live." Then, if she asks you to compare existential philosophy with Neolithic art, it's best for you to say, "Who is Richard Burton, anyhow? He's an Italian tenor, right?" Brace yourself. This will go on for an hour or more.

If the interviewer is a male, your job is easy. Be sure to get a male interviewer. The subject will be college sports and he'll do all the talking. You should say absolutely nothing. Just nod in agreement each time your interviewer tells you the coach is ruining the team. Who cares what team or what coach? Just smile and nod your head. Guys are predictable. They want to talk about sports. You see, university administrators have found only one way to communicate with the general public—through sports. So football and basketball are all the general public knows about college—males, especially.

Your future boss is part of the general public and associates college with sports. If you know sports, you'll do fine on your interview. If you're a woman being interviewed by a male corporate executive, he won't expect you to know diddily about sports. All the more reason for you to be a walking sports encyclopedia. It's not a bad idea to wear something real sexy, if you know what I mean. Sub-hip-hugger jeans might do the trick.

Before you go off for an interview, pay attention to the paragraph below. It's the transcript of my own job interview with Amalgamated Importers. No kidding. I recorded everything on a little vest-pocket tape recorder I got at Woolworths or Grants or somewhere. Lucky I got a guy to do the interview— a guy who was in my own fraternity, no less. The interview was a breeze. Here's the transcript. I seldom had to say a word during the interview, so you just see what the interviewer said and where I nodded. Pay attention real close:

O.K. Hector. Why do you think the Bulldogs lost eleven games last year? Aren't you embarrassed? (Nod). I certainly would be! You guys will never get into a bowl game losing eleven games. Don't you think it's high time for a new coach? (Nod). I don't know what the hell your athletic director is smoking. I would have fired the joker three years ago when he went 0 and 11 the first time. This year he lost a chance to beat Southeastern State Community College by blowing a fourth quarter field-goal attempt from thirteen yards. Never should have let Mahoney kick it from thirteen yards.

Mahoney missed five other kicks that game. Not one of the others was as far out as thirteen yards. They were all dinky chip shots. Everybody knows Mahoney has no range. Come on! (Enthusiastic nod).

Ok! Let's talk business. Say! You probably learned Chinese in your courses at State U., right. (Apologetic, negative nod). Oh! You didn't? Too bad. We're doing $340 million a year with China now. Well, no big deal. Our Hong Kong group handles most of the translations for us anyhow. You CAN do multiple-choice, I hope. (Confident nod). Way to go! Can you fill in the blanks? (Negative nod). Yeah! I know. They're all multiple-choice these days. But that's important to us--the M/C skills, I mean. We just can't hire new folks unless they have the M/C skills we're looking for. And it sure sounds like you've got 'em (Fig. 16.1).

You know, we've got eight Bulldogs right here in this branch of the company. You've probably seen them at the games. (Tentative nod). They never miss one. The company has a block of Bulldogs season tickets on the 50-yard line, right across from the student section. The guys sit right next to each other on the same row. Row six, I think. Each one has a huge red Bulldogs letter tattooed onto his chest. They're crazy guys! So they don't show up for work on Mondays. No big deal. They know how to talk sports with the clients and that's what counts. So, with your Bulldogs connections and all, you should fit in real good here. The guy who does the letter D for us, Sam, he's retiring from the company this year. He has been our regular D for ages. My God! I guess Sam's been with us thirty-nine years now. So we need a new D. How about it? You want to be a D? How's $286,000 to start? (Ambivalent, negotiating nod). You're not sure? Really? What's the problem? You're not chicken about the tattoo are you? (Negative nod). Well, that's good! You had me going there for a while. It's not the money is it? (Negative nod). O.K., you've got me. You drive a tough bargain. O.K! O.K! O.K! We'll throw in the Bulldogs season tickets for free. (Gleeful nod). Great! Good to have you on board. Sure, you can go back to Aruba for a couple more weeks. Maybe you'll want to get your D done in the islands. Let's say June 15 to start. That's way before football season begins. Lots of time! Wonderful! You'll like it here at Amalgamated. (Enthusiastic nod and secret fraternity hand shake).

William W. Ward

(Fig 16.1)

Chapter 17

Hector's Graduation Tips

Notes On How I Made It Through State U.

In my last semester of college, I started keeping a sort of diary. I was getting real worried about graduation on account of I didn't make it the first two times. Here's what I put in my diary:

At long last, graduation! It's been a helluva long haul, but I'm finally on the brink. If I can just pass those last five courses! When I started college seven years ago, it seemed like such a good idea to postpone all the killer courses until the last semester. Now the idea looks pretty dumb. I've been over and over my grade point average at least a dozen times. My TI-30 calculator keeps giving me the same number--1.97344889. Not a thousandth of a point higher. I've even considered doing calculations by hand. Hey! A college degree is important, but not that important. No way will I to go to the trouble of manual math. But a GPA of 1.97344889 is just not good enough. I need a 2.00000000 or I can't graduate. Last year and the year before I had to send forty-seven relatives back home unfulfilled. Boy were they pissed! Especially the second time. This is my last chance. They won't come again. How am I going to get my average to 2.00000000?

Can I pull a B in Diffident Equations? Not likely! Not when I got F's the last three times. What about NASDAQ Stock Tips? Not much chance there either. NASDAQ is not very tough, but I've got Professor Lars Sigfried Jose Ahamadahoolahanski for the second time. I still can't understand a word Dr. "Hoola" says. Looks like I'll need to boost my grades in French 422 (Escape from Moliere), Zoology 36D (Mammiferous Anatomy), and Ecology 001 (Planting Wierd Shrubs Over Smelly Old Landfills). But I've got C's going in each one. My TI-30 calculator tells me I need A's on three finals to finish with a 2.00000000 cumulative average. I've never rallied like this during finals. Never! Not once in seven years have I gotten A's on three finals! Damn, it's just two weeks before finals start. Gotta think fast.

Wait! This might work. If I can just squeeze a final grade of A in one course and C's in the others, I'll be over the top. Yep. It comes to exactly 2.00000001. Well, if I need an A, there's only time for one thing. I've got to play the pre-med card. Everybody says it works, but they're all bio majors. It will be hard to play the pre-med card when the only biology course I've taken is Mammiferous Anatomy. I've never even seen a fetal pig. I've never tracked down a single mutant fruit fly that escaped from the genetics lab only to squat on the department secretary's fruit-salad lunch and lay two hundred eggs. Well, I better sharpen my acting skills and drop the pre-med card on a professor who's really out of it. Someone not too good at English. It will have to be Professor "Hoola".

Like On "General Hospital"

"Uh, Professor 'Hoola.' I mean Ahamadahoolahanski. I wonder if you know I'm a pre-med? A pre-med! What? No! You're getting it confused with premeditation. No! That's not what I'm saying. Pre-med! You know--I want to study medicine. You know, medicine--like in pills. No! I don't have a headache. No! I don't need an aspirin. I'm fine. I just want to be a docter. You know, docter, D-O-C-T-E-R. Yes, I know you're a doctor. I don't mean that kind. I mean the MD kind. I want to make money. I want to be real rich. You know, MD. Right! Like on 'General Hospital.' Right! 'General Hospital.' So I need an A in NASDAQ Stock Tips. An A! An A! You know. A real high grade. An A! Start of the alphabet like in M/C tests. You know, an A. That's right! An A. You think you can do it? Do you think you can give me an A? You know? You think you can give me an A so I can get into medical school? Yeah! An A. Right. You can? Oh, that's great! That's great! Great! You know, like super! Yeah, super."

So, that's how I did it. That's how I finally graduated — using the pre-med card on Professor "Hoola." I don't think he had the foggiest idea what was going on, but I got the A.

Granola Pancake Breakfasts

It's party time! Your senior week in college will be like graduation night in high school. Except it's seven times longer. That's right. Seven days and seven nights of uninterrupted party. The college has things planned for the entire 168 hours. They have non-stop activities to keep you out of trouble. They've got everything from Barry Manilow and Wayne Newton concerts to granola pancake breakfasts and three-legged races. The whole thing has been planned from start to finish by thirty-six lesser assistant deans. The deans are really psyched. They even stay awake for seven days and nights to see it through. Usually fourteen students show up. The rest of you will go to Aruba. It's a bit dry in Aruba, but the rum flows like water. You'll come back with a raging hangover, a whole body tan, and lots of tattoos. You'll even get tattoos in places where you didn't know you had places. Tattoos are so cool. Skip the body piercing. They have no aesthetic sense in Aruba and it just won't turn out right. Body piercing has to be left to highly skilled artisans — like those fat, bearded, toothless, bare-chested Bohemians wearing black leather jeans and working out of run-down store-front shops in the Bronx.

Graduation Check List

Before you get too excited, check the official graduation list. If you've not paid all your parking fines, they won't put you on the list. All 1,726 graduating seniors will have dozens of unpaid parking fines. Each will try paying them off in person at the Parking Services building the week before graduation. Students will line up along the whole length of University Avenue trying to get to a single teller's window displaying a tiny "Out to Lunch" sign. Those poor students are in for a long wait. Lunch break for State U. Parking Services employees starts at noon on Monday and goes to about midday on Wednesday. If Monday is a holiday, everything shifts ahead twenty-four hours. So pay your fines early. You can't afford to waste time hanging out in long lines. There are more important things to do, like preparing for the graduation ceremony. There's lots of stuff to gather. If you want to do things right, you need every minute you can muster. Start with a checklist of things you want at graduation. It could be a long list. Table 17.1 lists just a few items you must not forget. Your own list could be much longer.

Table 17.1:
MUST ITEMS FOR GRADUATION

1. Gown
2. Mortar board and tassel
3. Underwear (optional)
4. Balloons, at least 50
5. Small helium canisters from chemistry lab
6. Beach balls (several large ones)
7. Compressed air horn
8. Champagne (three bottles — more if you're sharing)
9. Masking tape

The first two items are pretty much standard. If not properly clad (on the exterior) you won't be allowed to march at graduation. But underclothing is optional. The idea is to see how few clothes you can get away with under your nearly see-through paper gown. Underwear is prudent, but not strictly necessary. The less you wear underneath, the more applause you get as your natural silhouette pokes through the flimsy, paper graduation gown on your march across the stage (Fig. 17.1). The name of the game is to get as much attention as you can. Partial nudity is the easiest way there is to get attention. It's your last hurrah. Make the most of it!

It's Just Too Revolting

Everything else in Table 17.1 augments the spectacle you plan to create. You'll want to create a real big spectacle, so start collecting stuff months in advance — like giant balloons. Balloons are best inflated with small helium canisters you sneak out of chemistry lab. Take only canisters with the

Hey Doc! Does Speling Count?

(Fig 17.1)

abbreviation "He" on the label. That's helium. Whatever you do, don't take canisters with the abbreviation "She" on the label. That's hydrogen. Remember the Hindenburg? Not a good idea to fill balloons with hydrogen.

A few minutes before your name is called, inflate and tie off twenty or more balloons. As you climb the stairs to the platform, let the balloons loose, all but one. Inhale the contents of the remaining balloon just before you get your diploma from the dean. Inhaling helium is loads of fun, but inhaling hydrogen is risky, especially if you smoke. With lungs full of helium, you'll sound like the Christmas Chipmunks. Thank the dean in your new ultra-soprano voice. Be as loud as you can, so everyone hears. You'll get more attention than you could imagine. Even more attention than you got setting fire to the high school chemistry lab. O.K. So the fire wasn't your fault.

The beach balls are supposed to come out at the most serious part of the program. Put yours up in the air right away so they get bounced from student to student throughout the ceremony. You should have several spares in case your first few land on potted rose bushes and burst. In addition to balloons, most modern college graduations have eighty or ninety compressed air horns going pretty much non-stop. You know. The kind used to signal category five tornadoes in Nebraska or 800-foot tsunamis in Hawaii. Not every student will have one. But you certainly don't want to be left out. Check out your local Army/Navy store. They probably have lots of great air horns.

Champagne is a must during the graduation ceremony. No sober person ever wants to shake hands with a college dean. It's just too revolting. Take my advice. Get tanked! Finally you need a roll of masking tape. Use the tape to create clever messages on the top of your mortarboard and across the back of your gown. That's what newspaper photographers look for at college graduations—the most clever masking tape messages on hats and gowns. If you come up with something real clever, you could be the front-page feature in tomorrow's newspaper. Instant celebrity status—all based on masking tape. Table 17.2 suggests some great, time-honored and dignified masking tape messages.

Table 17.2:
HECTOR'S TIME-HONORED AND DIGNIFIED MASKING TAPE MESSAGES

1. College sucks
2. Hey! Ma. I done it!
3. Impeach W.
4. Disbar Clinton.
5. World. Here I come!
6. Look! Ma. No Branes.
7. Aruba or bust!
8. Hi, Mom. You're gonna love my new tongue stud. Bet you'll never guess where my boyfriend had his ring inserted.
9. Restore PPA 108
10. Trash Bin!
11. Bomb Saddam!
12. Dorm Porn Rules
13. Pop. Nobody wants to give me a job 'cause I got no marketable skills. All I can do are M/C tests. So I'm coming back home to live with you and your girlfriend. O.K?
14. Ban all Books
15. Eat Fresh Louisiana Catfish
16. All I learned in college was how to plant wierd shrubs over smelly old landfills
17. The State U. President is a lightweight
18. Ma, we finally got those poopy pigs out of our apartment. So where are the new linens you said you were going to ship?
19. We Have a Tulane President at a 4-Lane University
20. I am wearing absolutely nothing under this flimsy, paper gown. All the guys are hoping for rain.

No graduation gown or mortarboard is complete without at least fifty-six yards of masking tape speling out such clever statements. Buy one of those giant hurricane rolls at Home Depot.

Your Final Stroll

The whole idea of the graduation ceremony is to get attention. Don't let your presence slip by unnoticed. You need to prepare your guests as well as yourself. To mark your stroll across the graduation platform, give each of your relatives ear-piercing horns, ultrasound dog-whistles, and electronic noisemakers. The lower your rank in class (I was rock bottom), the more important this assault on the tympanic membrane becomes. Make the most of it!

Ancient Druid tradition requires that you dance a small jig as you accept your final passage into mature adulthood. You need to work on the jig during senior week in Aruba. Practice with the full set of helium balloons and air horns. To simulate the actual event, have a few drinks first. Practicing the jig is especially important if you've never caught a winning touchdown pass in the waning seconds of a nationally televised championship football game. Football wide receivers do real good jigs. Yours should be just as good. Your jig will be recorded on thousands of video cameras. Make the jig a good one!

Stonehenge and the Time of the Druids

The graduation ceremony is a solemn occasion. The ritual dates back to Stonehenge and the time of the Druids. The glee club sings of the glory of football games long past, when nobody wore helmets and everybody got knocked silly. There is a whole verse about contusions, concussions, and comas and about carrying unconscious players off the field. It's a real inspirational song. Later, when students begin their march to the podium, there's piped-in playing of "Pomp and Circumcision." It takes 2,436 verses, all exactly the same, to accompany the 1,726 students across the stage.

If your graduation is anything like mine, it will go about like this. First thing you notice as you enter are hundreds of college dignitaries and lesser luminaries decorating the stage. Now you know where your tuition money has been going—to light up the lives of lesser luminaries. The dean is desperately practicing the names of students he's never met. As the ceremony is about to start, he's still working on names beginning with V--four more letters to go. The senior associate lesser assistant dean is there with her fake China-doll smile. When I was a State U. student, she was the only administrator I ever met. She gave out the financial aid checks each month. I know she hated her job, but she was never without that nauseating smile.

Speaking of nauseating, the college president was there too. He stayed long enough to take his bow and then scurried off for his morning martini. A representative from the graduating class of 1911 was given a place of honor. His great-granddaughter was graduating. A retired stonemason, he was asked to say a word or two about the American work ethic. Wearing a real wooden mortarboard, symbol of his trade, he rambled on incoherently for fifty-seven minutes about the cheap mortar he had to use during the depression. He was never invited back.

God, Aruba, and Uvula Rings

There is the "Professor of the Year", chosen by the students because he gave out 542 A's in a class nobody bothered to attend. It's his eighth year as P.O.Y. There's the ecumenical chaplain wearing an eighteen-inch-long crucifix on a gold chain around his neck. He sports an oversized Star-of-David lapel pin on one side of his denim jacket and a six-inch-diameter McGovern/Eagleton presidential campaign button on the other side. His Moslem shawl nicely complements his hand-stitched Indian moccasins and coonskin cap. His secular blessing on the occasion carefully avoids all mention of God, Aruba, and uvula rings. A representative of the governing board looks bored as hell throughout the six-hour-long ordeal. She dozes off and I can tell she's even snoring. The guy to her left awakens her abruptly each time she is supposed to stand. Sixteen times. I counted.

Last year I went to the State U. graduation ceremony. Cliff's daughter was graduating. Graduation is pretty much as it was years ago. The main difference is lots more balloons, beach balls, and tsunami sirens. As always, a highlight is the appearance of the senior class president. The class president is chosen by the entire senior class. Two criteria are used. The class president has to look like Jay Leno and act like Eddy Murphy or the other way around. Druid tradition requires his speech to be twenty minutes of one-liners. The whole speech is campus humor. Students think it's hilarious, but nobody else gets the jokes. The senior class roars with laughter while 268 dignitaries sit in stone-faced silence. There could have been 269 dignitaries, but the morning martini has lured away the president. Presidents come and go, but some things never change.

Last comes the inspirational keynote speech. A self-made multimillionaire presents the speech. He says he now wishes he had finished 7th grade. He has donated so much money to the intercollegiate athletics program at State U. that almost every campus road bears his name. There's an Artimus J. Culpepper Boulevard, a Culpepper Drive, a Culpepper Court, a Culpepper Avenue, a Culpepper Circle, a Culpepper Road, a Culpepper Street, a

Culpepper Lane, a Rue de la Culpepper, and even an Artimus J. Culpepper Cul-de-sac. Would you believe, that block-long unpaved alley between the Physics Annex and the Health and Human Services building has now been named the Artimus J. Culpepper Trail. No wonder Federal Express never could get those care packages from Mom delivered to the right place.

Culpepper's speech is all about self-reliance, pioneer spirit, motivation, the value of hard work, and the God-given right for civilians to carry fully-loaded, semi-automatic, high-powered assault rifles around shopping malls and school yards. Most of his talk is about the value of having weapons. From the Good Book, he quotes chapter and verse about guns, assault rifles, and the right to bear arms. He's real knowledgeable. You'd almost think that him and Charlton Heston wrote the Good Book themselves. He finishes by reminiscing about all the great times he had as honorary colonel in the Louisiana State Militia. It's a super talk and everyone leaves feeling inspired and uplifted. The Colonel is my kind of guy.

Aside from all the gun stuff, what does Colonel Culpepper do for a living that takes him 138 minutes to describe in the thickest southern drawl y'all have ever heard? He's a catfish farmer. But there's more. Teaming up with a bunch of top-level administrators having unlimited access to a secret State U. slush fund, he's just landed a huge federal grant to build a commercial fish farm over a nearby smelly old landfill.

Section V

They Put Me on the State U. Board? I Can't Believe It!

Chapter 18

Heads Up on the Administration

Now I'm a Bulldog Threw and Threw

So after graduation, things worked out pretty good for me. I like being with Amalgamated Importers. They came threw with the $286,000 starting salary, just as promised, and Professor "Hoola's" stock tips have already earned me a cool thirty-three hundred grand on the NASDAQ. I've got a plush office and my own gorgeous secretary. She's real hot. Not bad for a guy who took seven years to graduate from college, and only then by the skin of my teeth. The fourteen-day return trip to Aruba was out of this world. But, oh my god, did my tattoo hurt. Sixteen hours of non-stop pain. Now, after several years, the big red D on my chest still itches like hell. It's probably from I have to shave every week so the D shows up real good at the games. The other guys told me the itching would go away in a few months. No way!

How I Got On the State U. Board

After three Bulldogs games, I became best friends with Jonathan, who does the second letter L, and Cliff, who does the O. Cliff is the biggest sports nut I've ever met. He's president of the Bulldogs Boosters, he's special alum advisor to the Intercollegiate Sports Marketing Department for State U., and he sits on the university Governing Board. On the Board, Cliff chairs the most influential committee--the Committee on Intercollegiate Athletics. Cliff is always talking about how important sports are for State U. Off season, when he's not too busy, me and Cliff talk all the time. Cliff's a fun guy. I thought I knew a lot about the university when I was a student. No way! Cliff knows so much more than I ever dreamed. He tells me just about everything.

When I started working for Amalgamated Importers, he told me how important it is for Amalgamated to have representatives on the State U. Board. It's a way to pull strings. In his eight years on the Board, Cliff has landed fourteen State U. contracts for Amalgamated. Cliff's inside information has gotten Amalgamated the lowest bid on everything from imported tractors for the agricultural experiment station to closed-circuit TV systems for the football clubhouse. Company profits are up 123% in just the past year. Cliff has had a lot to do with Amalgamated's good fortune. But the work got to be too much for him—all that influence peddling and stuff. He couldn't do it all. He really needed help on the inside and I was his guy. So Cliff started pulling even more political strings and, in no time at all, I was on the State U. governing board. Pretty neat (Fig. 18.1).

Public Beheadings

After I got on the State U. Board, Cliff gave me a little lesson on what the administration is really like. Here's some of the stuff he told me. As State U. evolved through the 1900's, so did its administrators. The State U. president began to recognize he has it real good. He has power, influence, prestige, and a Governing Board willing to let him make all decisions (see Chapter 21). He also likes the fact that State U. covers his every expense—for free. As the 20th century drew to a close, the State U. president became sort of a monarch—a return full cycle to the era that spawned Stata U. in the first place (see Chapter 4). Being college president is fun, but not nearly as much fun as being absolute monarch.

Even as monarchs, modern college presidents cannot order public beheadings of heretical professors as they did in the Middle Ages. All they can do is look back on those glorious days with nostalgia. Denied the grandeur of public executions of errant professors, today's university presidents must keep control in other ways. They do this by ignoring everybody and everything. They pay no attention to students and they ignore

(Fig. 18.1)

the faculty, the citizen-taxpayers, and the state's governing bodies. They don't do much of anything unless their actions focus attention on themselves. Me and Cliff don't like how the State U. president operates. For him, it's all a big show. But lots of legislators get fooled by the show and somehow they hold the State U. president in awe. He controls the legislature, the press, and the general public. Manufacturing an appearance is key to controlling the university. "Do nothing of value, but appear as if you have" is the unofficial motto of the modern university president, says Cliff. This motto also serves as a guideline for the lesser assistant administrators. At Board meetings, the president keeps saying, "Hey! This is working. Let's not change it."

Madison Avenue U

As university presidents of the 1980s and 1990s freed themselves from inside and outside influences, they consolidated even more power with fancy images of the university. Their fabricated images describe the university as a place of enlightenment, a home for free thought and free speech, and a safe haven for the underprivileged. What a bunch of bull crap. But there's more. To create and embellish these images, presidents needed lots more administrators, especially ones trained in public relations and law. So, in recent years, at taxpayer's expense, they've hired dozens of in-house speechwriters and PR experts to embellish their presidential images and lawyers to isolate them from challenges of mismanagement. The State U. president's new speechwriters do nothing but sing the praises of his administration while the PR staff creates glossy, multi-color fliers and brochures to advertise the university's image. Me and Cliff don't believe a word of it. With or without the PR, we're still the same old run-of-the-mill state university. A few ups, a few downs, and not much else.

Professorial Poster Persons

With the new focus on appearance, presidents of many state universities now pretend everything is wonderful--never been better. To do this, they've had to ignore reality and suppress criticism. Surrounding themselves with lots of lackey-lawyers and mindless yes-persons (YP's) has helped. But some of these YP-lackeys are the pits! They just go along with every dumb idea the president has, just to bolster his ego. The State U. president has a huge ego. He works hard on self-deception, blatant fabrication, and outright lying. So he fools himself into thinking he's doing a great job. Once I complained about some little thing the president had done—sort of a racial blunder in a speech, I think it was. Wow! Did I get my head handed to me! I won't do that again. From now on, I'm keeping my mouth shut. I like being on the Governing Board. So we let the State U. president do just about anything he pleases, racial blunders included. It works better this way.

The president expends enormous amounts of time, energy, and money trying to convince others that State U. is the greatest. Sure, it has its good points. At State U., and probably at other universities, there are small, isolated pockets of real education and high quality research. On the Board, we go along with the president to make excellence appear the norm instead of the rare exception. We help turn these isolated pockets of excellence into grossly embellished poster stories. They become centerpieces of the president's glossy, glitzy advertising campaigns—but only if the professorial poster person plays ball with the administration.

Professors not "on the team" get nowhere with this president. He works only with "team players" willing to "play the game" by his unpublished rules. He punishes the rest (see Chapter 20). He selects racially and ethnically balanced "team players" of dubious distinction who project onto him a politically correct image. Ironically, while fabricating such an image for himself, he tolerates no professor who talks about free speech, academic freedom, human rights, due process, democratic values, and the respect for rules of law. Some say the university is in moral decline. Some say standards of education and educational accomplishments are dropping. Who's to know? Maybe the cartoon characters, Frank and Ernest, had it right. Both are sitting on a park bench while Frank is reading a book entitled "Self Improvement." In answer to an apparent question from Ernest, Frank summarizes the contents of the book by saying, "The idea is to stay the same while everyone else gets worse."

Administratium

As university presidents have isolated themselves more and more from students and faculty, they have become the butts of campus humor in newspaper editorials and protest rallies. A favorite way to mock the State U. president is with a description of the mysterious element, Administratium. Here's what appeared in one editorial:

SCIENTISTS DISCOVER NEW ELEMENT: ADMINISTRATIUM

The heaviest element known to science was recently discovered. The element, tentatively named Administratium (Ad), has no protons or electrons, which means that it has atomic number 0 and falls outside the natural patterns exhibited by other elements. However, it does have one neutron, 125 assistants to the neutron, 75 vice-neutrons, and 111 assistants to the vice-neutrons. This gives it an atomic mass of 312. The 312 particles are held together by a force involving the continuous exchange of mesa-like particles called "memos." Because it has no protons or electrons, Administratium is inert. Nontheless, it can be detected chemically, in that it seems to impede every reaction in which it is present. According to one of the discoverers, even a small amount of Administratium made one reaction that normally lasts less than a second, take more than four days. Administratium has a half-life of approximately three years. It does not actually decay. Instead, it undergoes a reorganization in which a vice-neutron, assistants to the vice-neutron, and certain assistants to the neutron exchange places. Some studies have indicated that its mass actually increases after each reorganization, although this is yet to be explained. Another phenomenon that has been observed, as expected from the mechanics of the minute particles, is that the more one tries to pin down the positions of vice-neutrons within the structure of Administratium, the more uncertain those positions become.

High-Tech Era

To take attention away from a system he's gotten all screwed up, the State U. president claims to be promoting and advancing the frontiers of high-tech research. He constantly ballyhoos the slightest State U. advances in science, technology, engineering, medicine, agriculture, biotechnology, and computer science. Like, he's got this stupid center telling him that mega-doses of plain old black licorice can cure cancer, hangnails, anxiety, irritable bowel syndrome, and just about every disease known to man. So he throws tons of money at the CCCC (the Cancer Cure Candy Center). It's not clear from their publication record that they do any college-level research at the CCCC. I mean, all their "journal articles" come out in "Prevention" magazine—you know, the one at the grocery store check-out counter right next to "National Enquirer" and "Star."

Then he's got another center that does nothing at all but plant wierd shrubs over smelly old landfills. It's called the Center For Planting Wierd Shrubs Over Smelly Old Landfills (the CFPWSOSOL). Who knows why the CFPWSOSOL would do this stuff and who knows why anyone would pay them good money for such a project? Yet the president pulls out all the stops to fund the CFPWSOSOL. Under orders from the president, the Board has approved a new option in the Ecology major at State U. It will be called "Planting Wierd Shrubs Over Smelly Old Landfills." You can guess how me and Cliff voted on this one.

But it just gets worse. The president props up this idiot professor who studies how jellyfish glow in the dark. No project could possibly be dumber than that one. I mean, really! There cannot be a single practical application for such an idiotic research project. Not one! But the president seems to like the jellyfish professor and throws all kinds of money at that dumb jellyfish professor. Nobody can figure out why there is so much State U. support for such a useless project. The jellyfish professor must be saying and doing all the right things to get extra special treatment from the president. He must be the best "team player" State U. has ever seen. Either he's a super "team player" who butters up the president at every opportunity or there's a little bit of extortion or hanky-panky going on. We don't know. So, when it comes to funding stupid jellyfish projects, the State U. treasury is a bottomless pit. I mean, the slime-ball jellyfish get millions of dollars every year.

Once the president finishes throwing money around for all his pet research projects (like black licorice, smelly old landfills, and slime-ball jellyfish), there's nothing much left. So to keep the place from plunging into the red, he orders the cheapest chalk he can find for the classrooms—you know, the kind of chalk with little pieces of sand and gravel scattered throughout. This gravel-chalk makes that awful scratching sound on the blackboard and it leaves a permanent record of scratch marks on the blackboards so you can read the whole semester's lectures at one time. Then he finds cheap toilet paper that's sort of transparent waxed paper and he orders that cheap brand for the whole university. No way am I going to use that stuff. So every time I have to come in for a Board meeting, I bring my own "Squeezably Soft" Charmin toilet paper from home.

When the custodians want more than a 0.1 percent salary increase, he fires the whole lot of them and hands out dust rags to professors so they can dust away bat droppings and sewer pipe drippings from their desks and lab benches. He's not willing to pay custodians $6.25 an hour if he can get the professors to do the work. This is no joke! He really issued dust rags to the professors. So, with no money left (after black licorice and smelly old landfills and slime-ball jellyfish get theirs), the place just about grinds to a halt. Nothing gets fixed, nothing gets repaired, and all the buildings are allowed to crumble into the ground. The most neglected ones are the dorms, apartments, lecture rooms, and teaching labs—the buildings that matter most to the students. Each building gets a coat of cheap paint every seventy-five years, whether it needs it or not. That's about it for maintenance. Well, at least there is the "12-inch rule."

Pompous Protection of the Personal Posterior

The president made us pass the "12-inch rule" at a Board meeting last year. O.K. You probably never heard of the "12-inch rule." Not all universities have a "12-inch rule." But State U. does. It's one of our proudest accomplishments. Let me give you some background.

You see, lots of complaints come into the State U. Facilities and Maintenance Department. An ex-sergeant, dishonorably discharged for being too autocratic for the military, now runs this State U. department. Once a military person has been discharged for autocratic offenses, that person has only one career recourse. He or she must become the director of a University Facilities and Maintenance Department. The State U. Director of Facilities and Maintenance was not only discharged by the army, but was rejected by thirty-seven other state universities before we picked her up. To remain totally domineering, her only skill, she engages in a paramilitary practice known as PPPP--Pompous Protection of the Personal Posterior. More crudely put, the director covers her ass at all times.

PPPP means that no mistake is ever the fault of the Director of Facilities and Maintenance. She is never responsible for any boondoggles, no matter how large, no matter how small. It is always someone else's fault. Despite this PPPP doctrine of administrative infallibility, all sorts of bad things happen within the buildings and around the grounds at State U. You know, little things like ten dorm toilets overflowing simultaneously in the hallways for a day and a half. Make no mistake. The massive dormitory flood that ensued in this case had nothing to do with faulty plumbing or poor maintenance. Such a disaster must never implicate the director. Others are to blame. Never is the director responsible for anything bad that happens at State U.

Then there was the time a bunch of 800-pound agricultural Experiment Station pigs broke into a co-ed's apartment, ransacked her closet, smashed her entertainment center, and then pooped all over her bed. Based on PPPP, there was no connection between this event and a huge breach in the termite-riddled wooden fences surrounding the Experiment Station pig farm. No connection at all. It is unfortunate that the poopy bed ruined a perfectly good affair between the co-ed and her favorite hunk—a 373-pound State U. football jock. This was a particularly messy problem. Naturally, the Director of Facilities and Maintenance sidestepped the whole pig-poop incident, she invoked PPPP, and she officially blamed the co-ed for maintaining an attractive nuisance in her apartment.

These kinds of events are common. Sometimes huge blackboards fall off the walls and smash into tiny bits on the floor—the act of a loving god, as students get a whole week off from classes. Sometimes roofs collapse on lecture halls filled with 632 students—not such a loving act. Little things like these happen all the time—never traceable, of course, to the maintenance department. But the president has cut back maintenance budgets so much (because of black licorice, smelly old landfills, and slime-ball jellyfish) that the director must be very selective about how and when she mobilizes her staff. She loves this awesome power. Budget cutbacks mean she can wield an iron fist, denying ninety-eight percent of all emergency calls. She loves the power to set priorities. Pig poop is not on her priority list. I know. I saw the list one time. So be sure to come to college with several sets of bed linens or an aggie boyfriend who's used to such porcine inconveniences.

First priority for the maintenance department is a building on fire. Maintenance tries to do something about buildings ablaze, especially a building occupied at the time by 632 students. Usually the crew arrives on the very next day, even if it means missing their lunch hour break. Now that's what I call responsive bureaucracy.

Second priority is a flood at least twelve inches deep. That's where the "12-inch rule" comes into play. The president got us to pass the "12-inch rule" at a Board meeting last year. So now, if your dorm or apartment gets flooded real bad, say with backed up raw sewage, the maintenance people will require you to show up in person at the maintenance building to fill out a preliminary flood report in triplicate (they still use carbon paper). If you fill out each line just right, they will issue you a six-inch, ten-cent plastic ruler. Before you can get the ruler, you need to make a five-dollar deposit. You must pay a part-time cashier who's available from noon until 1:30 p.m. in a building nearly a mile away. After you make payment, you must return another mile to get the ruler. Once you get the official ruler, the maintenance staff will ask you to monitor the depth of the sewage until it gets to twelve inches.

It's a little tricky measuring twelve inches of raw sewage with a six-inch ruler. But after a while you'll get the hang of it. When the level reaches twelve inches, you're allowed to submit a final report in person—same building where you got the ruler, but in a completely different wing several floors up. Usually they think you are exaggerating, so they'll ignore a twelve-inch flood claim. It's best to claim the sewage is fifteen inches deep. If you want your five dollars back, you have to return the ruler in person (different office, opposite side of campus) and fill out the official ruler deposit return form (the RDRF). A five-dollar refund check will be mailed to your home several months after you graduate. At State U. this form is always called the RDRF. Use this abbreviation or the maintenance receptionist will have no idea what you're talking about. Once the report is properly processed, the maintenance crew will show up in a week to ten days. Perhaps they will do something about the sewage flood—that has risen to twenty-one inches in the meantime. Usually they just evaluate the situation and leave for good. Who the hell wants to clean up raw sewage? That's what the "12-inch rule" requires— proper evaluation followed by prompt departure.

So, if you find yourself wading through twenty-one inches of raw sewage in the first week of classes, don't let it get you down. It could be worse. After all, there are practical solutions. The CCCC (Cancer Cure Candy Center) has a remedy for raw sewage spills. Just gulp down a whole 64-ounce box of black licorice in one giant swallow. All your problems and concerns will be purged like magic. By the way, that guy who does the landfill thing may want you to donate your dorm sewage so he can fertilize his wierd shrubs. Now that's progressive ecology for you.

Well, that was fun. But I digressed a bit. Back to our beloved State U. president. The State U. president thrives on self-serving, ribbon-cutting ceremonies that open new centers, bureaus, and institutes, especially ones about black licorice, smelly old landfills, or slime-ball jellyfish. That's why he's never available. He's always wielding ribbon-cutting scissors somewhere and getting his mug shot in every campus publication. Despite the effort of several full-time, state-supported personal trainers and make-up artists, the State U. president is not very photogenic. The black shoe polish he smears all over his hair (reluctantly, since his "Kiwi Proposal" failed and he must foot the bill himself) looks kind of tacky. Someone should tell him we all laugh behind his back. If he knew what a laughing stock he's become, he'd go back to his natural, glistening white hair and save all those Kiwi expenses.

So, back to ribbon cutting. The centers he keeps opening drain cash from other campus activities, even football (now this starts to get personal for me and Cliff). In other words, centers of learning undermine the very learning that they are supposed to provide. But the State U. president doesn't care. He cares only about appearance (like jet black hair). Maybe that's why we keep losing football and basketball games. The president only promotes the appearance of an athletic program.

What's Wrong with this Picture?

You are probably saying to yourself, "Oh, my God! What a sick picture of the university! Why didn't Mom and Dad tell me what's going on at State U? My grandfather went to State U. Why didn't he say something? This is terrible! Maybe I should drop out of college and become a catfish farmer. Perhaps I should make a career out of mutilating dimes and quarters and selling the coin-remains as tacky jewelry at small town street fairs."

Well, catfish farming and currency mutilation are certainly very attractive alternatives. But don't despair. What I described here is real good news for those in college. That's because it means you can get through college with almost no effort at all. At least no scholastic effort. College administrators will require very little from you as a student. They are far too busy putting up a phony front. This is the plus side. But you will have to work at a fast-food franchise restaurant forty hours a week each semester and sixty hours a week each summer to pay your ever-increasing tuition. Someone has to subsidize the president's public relations flacks. Limit yourself to forty hours of hamburger slinging. You need plenty of time to go to State U. football and basketball games. After all, that's where most of your tuition dollars go--to finance the college intercollegiate athletic programs. You may as well take advantage of all that great entertainment, even if State U. loses almost every game it plays by scores like 83 to 6.

Cheeseburger, Cheeseburger, Cheeseburger

But, flipping several hundred-million burgers, freezing your butt off at countless football games, and becoming legally deaf from the roar at several hundred basketball games are small sacrifices. (I'm sorry. What did you just say?) You will surely be getting a six-figure salary as soon as you graduate from college. Hey! That's what I got right away. A cool $286,000 (see Chapter 16). We won't tell your future employer that all you learned at State U. was how to keep a few points above the absolute bottom of the grading curve (see Chapters 10 and 11) and how to make cheeseburgers real good. So long as your employer never finds out that students who got their college degrees in Angola, Bangladesh, or Madagascar actually learned something, you've got a secure future. But, just in case a graduate of the Zimbabwe Junior College of Metallurgy, Metaphysics, and Mysticism appears on your work scene with better credentials than you, keep those cheeseburger skills handy.

CHAPTER 19

THE UNIVERSITY AS A TAX-SUPPORTED MINOR LEAGUE FOR THE NFL AND NBA

Athletic Supporters

The American university is real important. Everyone knows this. It gets high school graduates educated so they can get good jobs. But there are so many other roles the university plays. Now that I'm on the Governing Board, I have learned about these other roles. Cliff has been a big help. He's shown me how education is just a small part of the big picture. The big picture is sports. Cliff and the State U. president don't agree about much, but they agree on one thing—State U. is all about sports. In the fall, the State U. president directs campus activities around football. In the winter, around basketball. University presidents like thinking of themselves as athletic supporters. They're real talented this way.

By being athletic supporters, university presidents sort of work for the National Football League (NFL) and the National Basketball Association (NBA). You might call American universities the minor league system for the NFL and NBA. It's not like baseball with a professional minor league system.

Professional baseball teams pay out lots of their own money to develop young talent. But professional football and basketball teams pay no development costs. They get seasoned athletes for free from American colleges and universities. While the pro leagues pay nothing, colleges and universities fork over tons of money to develop young athletes. Then, after four years, they hand the athletes over to pro leagues for nothing.

Development money actually comes from taxpayers and tuition payers who think their dollars are going toward education. No way! The money doesn't go for education despite what most people think. Cliff told me this is just a hoax. Universities collect tuition dollars to subsidize the NFL and the NBA. But this is a real good deal for us guys on the Board. The pros give out loads of free football and basketball tickets to everybody who's important. The important guys are university administrators, Governing Board members (like me and Cliff), influential alumni, friendly industrialists, and members of the state legislature. Already, I have twenty-two NFL season tickets--ten from Amalgamated and twelve from the State U. Board. My friends are all jealous as hell. I just say, "Hey, don't look at me. My friend Cliff has more than fifty season tickets."

Even though State U. loses nearly all its games, this doesn't seem to matter. Money just keeps flowing. When State U. wins, like back in the 1960's when we won two games, it's great. State U. even got into a bowl game one time back in the 1930's. With victory comes even more money. The president and state leaders take the credit for every victory. The president is real good at taking credit, even when he does nothing at all — that's most of the time.

Spies in the Locker Room

On rare occasions, when State U. wins a football or basketball game, alumni pour in lots of money to the university. Same thing with the state legislature. Fans from everywhere dump money into the university economy when State U. teams get on a roll — you know, like one victory in a row. These days, State U. seldom wins one game in a season, let alone one game in a row. We almost never get into bowl games or year-end tournaments. But other university teams do. With post-season contests, these teams get more attention, more crowds, and more television revenues than the also-rans. We're tired of being also-rans at State U. We want big, moneymaking athletic teams. Me and Cliff, we're working on this. Any money that State U. teams generate is rolled right back into the athletics program to make it bigger and better. Cliff's committee keeps all sports revenue in the program. He makes damn sure sports money is never used to fix up ramshackle old teaching buildings and such.

Sports money at State U. is used to reward successful athletes with plush housing facilities, fancy locker rooms, and super-modern clubhouses that resemble the Taj Mahal. The Taj Mahal, by the way, is a very old, world-famous casino in China or Utah or Finland — I don't remember which. But I know the Taj Mahal has lots of topless chorus girls. That's why State U. administrators have so many meetings there — they need the right ambiance to plan for our sports buildup. We may not win games at State U., but our sports facilities are world class, our coaches are treated like royalty, and our administrators have a great time with the "ambiance girls."

Within State U.'s super-modern clubhouse is a thirteen-million-dollar, 24-hour-per-day electronic surveillance system (imported by Amalgamated) following every move of every major college football team. We're tied in to about eighteen spy satellites, so we've got the whole western hemisphere covered. Nowhere in the world is spying so advanced. We pick up football formations U-2 spy planes cannot even see.

I'll give you an example. Last week, from hundreds of miles above the atmosphere, our satellite-based surveillance system recorded how many times a second-string wide receiver for the University of Idaho sneezed on the sidelines in a game against Washington State. It was four times. The State U. head coach thinks the wide-out was signaling for a new offensive line formation. Several of our assistant coaches have been studying that sneeze signal all weekend. I've been right alongside to offer my assistance. But, despite five camera angles, we can't tell if the sneeze was a true signal.

So, at $1500 per hour, we brought in an allergist (one of those STD poison ivy guys from the State U. medical center) to help us determine if the sneeze was a real signal or just a case of hay fever. He'll be studying the tapes for the next several weeks. He hopes to have a clear diagnosis before State U. comes up against Idaho next month. So this just shows you how useful the surveillance system is for our State U. football program. It's real essential.

By the way, we're now developing a State U. major in remote sensing for football surveillance. It will be a great major. The major will be called "Remote Sensing for Football Surveillance." You might want to specialize in this field. Just look it up on the State U. website. Click on the heading "New Academic Programs" and then look for "Remote Sensing for Football Surveillance," alphabetically listed under R. If you get lost, you can find "Remote Sensing for Football Surveillance" right next to "Retrofitting Smelly

Old Landfills into Catfish Aquaculture Facilities."

State U.'s surveillance facilities are so modern the CIA and intelligence divisions of the U.S. military have gotten interested. Their units have placed, in the State U. locker rooms and clubhouses, dozens of seasoned operatives (Fig. 19.1). With their perfectly tailored three-piece suits, these guys (sometimes the CIA "guys" are girls) are fun to watch as they scurry about locker rooms filled with brawny, stark-naked men, proudly displaying their masculinity. I took a bunch of pictures one day. They're real funny—maybe I'll use them in another book. How about "Chippendale Jocks Meet the CIA?" I like that title. The operatives snoop about day and night, intently and jealously studying the equipment they see in the men's locker room—the electronic surveillance equipment, I'm talking about, of course. These operatives hope to have similar equipment (oops) of their own some day. "Dream on!" Cliff says. "You guys get me the money and Amalgamated will get you the equipment."

Misplaced Placekicks

In off years, when a few placekicks bounce off the uprights, a football or two get fumbled at the goal line, or a seven foot, eight inch basketball point-guard fails six of his five courses, whole coaching staffs are fired at the end of the season. Cliff consults with the president all the time about these important staffing decisions. Except for games, I hardly get to see Cliff during football season. He's always meeting with the president about one sports crisis or another. Sometimes the crisis is a mass firing of an entire coaching staff in the second year of their five-year contracts. Sometimes it's near the start of seven-year contracts. This is not real good because millions of dollars continue to be paid out to the fired coaching staffs. If the hapless university lawyers get lucky, they find loopholes (sort of the way a drunk driver finds potholes in the road at night—no skills needed) and they break contracts with the fired coaches. But this doesn't happen often. Cliff says the State U. lawyers couldn't punch their way through a wet paper bag. In fact, our sports program attracts hundreds of stand-up comedians who flock to State U. to watch our university lawyers in action. They come here to find new material for lawyer jokes. Apparently we have the best material in the country—a huge number of lawyers and not one of them any good. State U. lawyers blow almost every case, so the university must pay off huge multi-year contracts to fired coaches, while new coaching staffs take over at even higher salaries.

(Fig. 19.1)

It is not uncommon for a big-name state university like ours to pay for three sets of football coaches and three sets of basketball coaches at the same time. State U. is going through this problem right now. It's beginning to look like that new basketball coach will have to be canned at the end of this season. Not a conference game in the win column and we're more than halfway through the season. He seemed so great when we signed him to a seven-figure, five-year contract with us a year ago. But now he can't seem to get anything working on the court. Well, these things happen. So we'll just can the coach and start over.

Displaced Administrators and Closeted Skeletons

It's not just coaches who get fired and then paid off. The same thing happens with State U. administrators. When an administrator is kicked downstairs, he or she is set up for life with a cushy faculty position requiring no teaching and no research. Ousted administrators get the best offices and the biggest salaries at the university, yet many of these demoted deans, presidents, and vice presidents don't even show up for work.

We've got this one guy who was fired from the position of Director of the Agricultural Experiment Station more than a decade ago. He's still on the payroll, but he hasn't been seen in more than ten years. He teaches nothing and does no research. But he orders thousands of dollars worth of equipment at State U. expense for an unused lab at some remote outpost—sort of a State U. "Siberia." He continues getting a quarter-million-dollar salary and a secret home mortgage supplement for life.

Why does State U. continue paying off these ex-administrators? Is it to reward them for years of dedicated service? No. Is it because they are useful as elder statespersons to guide the new administration? No. Is it because they help maintain the continuity of statewide university diplomacy? No. Is it for simple humanitarian reasons? No. The reason is much more basic. The current administration pays off ex-administrators so they'll keep their mouths shut.

Ex-administrators know all the State U. dirt. They know where the skeletons are hidden. They know, for a fact, that State U. keeps two sets of accounting books. They know which administrators have dipped into State U. slush funds to finance their own private economic ventures on the outside. They know who has broken laws and who has blatantly violated policies. They know who should be doing hard time. Worst of all, they know the shady dealings, misdeeds, and criminal acts of the current lot of administrators. They are very dangerous people. So deals are struck, hush money is delivered, and State U. skeletons remain in their smelly old closets.

Diverting the Teaching Budget

Since State U. fires so many coaches and so many administrators, we need smart Governing Board members to fix the problems. Cliff specializes in handling problems associated with the turnover of coaches. He's great at this job, especially when money gets tight. Tight money problems occur when we have too many fired coaches drawing full salaries at the same time. Sometimes we don't have enough money in the athletics budget to handle these emergencies. So Cliff finds ways to divert general teaching money into the athletics program. This way we can keep things going in the sports program. If Cliff diverts enough money, we can pay off all the fired coaches while extracting better coaches from other universities. Yeah, diverting education money into intercollegiate sports is illegal. We know this. But we keep it secret with our double accounting. We never get caught cooking the books because State U. has retained the same auditing firm for thirty years. It's a Scandinavian name—the auditing firm, that is. Something like Albertsen or Andersen, as I recall.

The auditors come up with clever ideas so that nobody can trace how much State U. money goes for sports. Like new sod for the football field ($585,000) is listed as "Agricultural Experiment Station—Turfgrass Field Testing." The imported center-cut oak flooring for the gymnasium ($883,000) is listed under "Forest Products Research Initiatives." New football helmets ($337,600) are placed under the banner of "University Capital Improvements." Special tutoring for college athletes ($2,454,400) is grouped with "Remedial Instruction—English as a Foreign Language." Football recruiting expenses ($3,675,000) are listed as "University Outreach Services." The best trick the auditors play is hiding the thirty-five secret home mortgage subsidies for the coaches and assistant coaches. This $1,875,000 annual expense comes under "Interest on Bonded Indebtedness." The auditors know how to play these games and they never expose the real set of books to the public. Everything is carefully concealed. Why risk their jobs?

A new coach may run a million-five or more, not including the thirty-year secret home mortgage subsidy and the new red and gold Jaguar each year. But this is just the start. New coaches come with a dozen or more high-priced assistant coaches who also need fancy new red and gold sports cars and secret home mortgages. Together, the coaches demand improvements in the State U. athletic facilities. Our last head football coach was real demanding. He wanted the whole place turned upside down. We had no choice, so we did what he wanted. Cliff got the assignment.

Cliff got State U. to sink millions of dollars into an all-weather, domed practice field. The new coach insisted on a red and gold dome—one that people could see from miles away. Those colors cost twice as much as the environmentally sensitive blue-gray material. But Cliff got a five-percent discount on a red and gold dome through Amalgamated. The dome was just the beginning. After this, Cliff refurbished locker rooms, clubhouses, and weight and training rooms. He doubled the stadium seating capacity. Why, I don't know. The stadium lies empty almost every day of the year—even when State U. has a game. We lose so many games that the fans have quit coming. But the stadium has other great uses. Like college kids keep breaking into the stadium to launch fire balloons (see Chapter 3). That's when the field is put to its best use.

Despite suffering countless dismal seasons with more head coaches than football victories, Cliff never stops trying to build up sports at State U. He recently put together a new, Madison Avenue-style advertising campaign to bolster the alumni power base, to help with athlete recruiting, and to build momentum for the new coaching staff. Cliff did it all. He knows so much about sports marketing. By the time Cliff got through, our dummy president had no idea what hit him. None of the expense accounting ever made it to the real set of books, so nobody knows what this sports buildup actually cost. But double bookkeeping is just good, clean business practice.

MOLDY-TOV's

During football rebuilding years, sometimes lasting a decade or two, bills pile up. The only way to pay these bills is to move money from general university funds into the athletics program. Every year it's another battle with State U. professors who want money to buy new research toys, like MOLDY-TOVS and MNR machines. You've probably never heard the word MOLDY-TOV (see Chapter 20). It's a kind of mess spectrometer—a Matrix Occluded Laser Dissolved Ytterbium—Time Or Velocity mess spectrometer to be exact. Well, I may have the name just a bit wrong. The professor who told me about MOLDY-TOV's doesn't speak no English too good. I'm not even sure what an MNR machine is—I think the letters stand for Magnetic Neucular Residents, or some such thing. But how many MOLDY-TOVS and MNR's does one university need, for god's sake? And it's not just research toys they ask for. The professors keep telling us to renovate zillions of shabby old teaching buildings. Those buildings are such eyesores! Buildings that ugly hurt the coaches' recruiting efforts. Most of us on the Board can't wait until the termites finish them off. Then we can put in a bunch of shiny new trailers for classrooms. Amalgamated Importers knows where to get real cheap trailers—you know, the ones with walls made of heavy-gauge aluminum foil. We've got these units all over campus now. It spruces up the place to have shiny trailers around. Sort of classy, like a mobile home park in the center of an abandoned Arkansas strip mine.

We can't do everything just the way the professors want. We've got more important issues. So we just say to the professors, "Go take a hike." Cliff's committee needs money to build up the sports program. Fortunately, Cliff and the president always win this battle against the faculty. Sports it is. This is the only subject about which Cliff and the president see eye-to-eye. They work close together to keep money flowing. They do it with new state taxes, increased student tuition and fees, and bulging student enrollment. This new money helps fill the general university coffers. Then Cliff empties the coffers into the sports programs.

To further balance the budget, we jam extra students into the classrooms and we get rid of a bunch of faculty we don't really need. Faculty are too liberal anyhow—just like all the radio talk shows say. Who needs liberal professors? We slash departmental budgets, roll back building maintenance, and cut teaching allocations. We've been doing all these revenue things at State U. for years. That's how come the classrooms are bursting at the seams. Not much we can do about this. We need all those tuition dollars. We're hard at work getting rid of lots more professors, especially the troublemakers. We call the purging process "Post-Tenure Review" to hide our real intent. The real intention of "Post Tenure Review" is to help us get rid of tenure. Once we get rid of tenure, we can dump a bunch more liberal, troublemaking, deadwood professors. Cliff says deadwood is not the right word. He calls these professors petrified wood. Belt-tightening is tough work for Board members, especially for people as fat as Cliff. That's just a little joke on Cliff. Hope he doesn't get pissed off.

Don't let me scare you. Even if everything sounds bad, it's not. All this stuff is real good news for students. During football-rebuilding decades, when administrators are squeezing the budget and gunning for deadwood professors, nobody pays attention to the students. Everything is sports, sports, sports. During such a fiscal crisis, drama of all sorts plays out behind the scenes. Administrators intimidate the professors with threats of "Post Tenure Review" purges, huge salary reductions, program consolidations that leave professors without home departments, and elimination of health coverage and fringe benefits.

Modern professors are always scared. Like they worry that some overly zealous administrator will accuse them of inciting students out of their 1950's-style apathy and lethargy into a life of activism. Activism is bad news, especially activism directed at the State U. administration. In front of hundreds of naïve students, professors can advocate violent overthrow of U.S. democracy. That's O.K. They could champion communism, pedophilia, legalized drugs, organized crime, and prostitution. Not a problem here, either. But the one subject that's taboo at State U. is revealing the truth about State U. mismanagement.

If a professor should tell students what really goes on in the State U. administration, the students could, heaven forbid, demand administrative reforms. This cannot be permitted. So inciting students to question the administration brings instant retaliation against both students and professors. The State U. president won't put up with anti-administration student activists or professors who encourage them. Cliff says, "Our president will crush the bastards." So most professors, unwilling to risk their precious security, shrink and cower under threats of administrative repression and retaliation. It's gotten so repressive here that professors fear the president's learning how they voted in the last general election. Most faculty are Democrats, but administrators don't like Democrats. Why should we, we're big businessmen? Once the administration attaches a liberal Democrat label to a professor, it's easy for the president to fire the professor under the new "Post Tenure Review" purge procedures. So professors are scared to death of the administration. They are so insecure that they lose their focus and they can't concentrate on teaching. As a result, they don't make you study and they give you those stupid M/C tests all the time.

You can't study for an M/C test—you just guess. So, with nothing but M/C tests, there's really no work for you to do. That's how I slipped by in just seven years—a lot of lucky guesses on M/C tests. In fact, I hardly ever went to class. Why bother? Nobody checks. Professors couldn't check even if they wanted. The classes are too big and the professors can't read the rosters (they're in English). Imagine a professor who speaks no English (see Chapter 3) trying to take roll in a classroom with 632 students.

A Whole Lot More Than We Can Afford

Few university intercollegiate athletics programs make a profit over and above the cost of maintaining the program. Very few, in fact, break even. At a State U. Board meeting, I learned the number of income-generating athletics programs in the country. Three! Cliff told me not to let the word get around, so you should just ignore this part of the book. (If you quote me, I'll deny I ever said it. That's what we do on the Board. We deny anything we've previously said or done.) Anyhow, people like to believe that college football earns money. They just cannot accept the idea that so much tax money goes to waste. I'm still having a hard time with the idea. I always thought big-time football schools made loads of money. I asked Cliff again and again. "Yes, Heck." (Cliff always calls me Heck.) "Only three university sports programs turn a profit. Just three."

Wow! The rest lose money, including State U. We lose a lot! It's still hard for me to believe this! But the important thing, Cliff says, is to keep this information secret. That's why the two sets of accounting books, you see? Cliff seems to have no idea just how much money we lose on sports. It's a secret, even from him. If he knows anything, he certainly isn't telling me. Even real pesky newspaper reporters can't seem to find out how much money State U. spends on football and basketball programs. They never get to see the real set of books. Legislators don't care, so long as they get re-elected and so long as those NFL tickets on the 50-yard line keep coming. The best estimate of football and basketball spending at State U. is a whole lot more than we can afford.

Your Stake in the NFL and NBA

Throughout the country, the amount of tuition and taxpayer money used to subsidize NFL/NBA minor leagues is staggering. At one Board meeting I learned it takes an average of $29.37 million in tax and tuition dollars to develop just one successful NFL player. This is just the up-front cost. More money comes from parents, alumni, and other state residents who fork over cash to watch university NFL/NBA minor league teams in action. This silent subsidy goes on week after week and year after year from coast to coast. It's a good thing I get all those free tickets. Otherwise I might be tempted to vote against the new coach's salary package. If it weren't for all those free tickets, I might even vote to drop State U. from Division 1A.

You know, we never win games against Division 1A teams so I wonder why we stay in a division way over our heads. But I do like those free NFL and NBA tickets. That's reason enough for me. The owners of professional teams in the NFL and NBA think this relationship with universities is real good. Their entire minor league systems cost them nothing. Some jocks even graduate from college. A few get a bit of education along the way so they're smart enough to become sports color commentators or used car salesmen after their playing years are over. It's a real good system for them too.

Then there are a few snooty universities like MIT, Columbia, or Berkeley. They just care about teaching and research. Boring! Their football teams are so bad they should be playing in a high school conference or something. Good thing we have a sports president at State U. who likes big-time football and basketball. We'd hate to be stuck with a wimpy reputation like MIT, Columbia, or Berkeley.

CHAPTER 20

STATE U, INCORPORATED

Two Sets of Books

Since I've been on the State U. board, everything has been business talk. We talk about money, profit, return on investment, cutting costs, and sports. This is just the way we do things at Amalgamated. Cliff says this has been going on for years. The state legislature keeps cutting back on appropriations for higher education, putting pressure on the Board to be fiscally responsible. I see this pressure at every Board meeting. Aside from football, we just talk about ways to make money and ways to cut costs. But Cliff says universities lag far behind regular businesses in developing corporate-style infrastructures. To catch up, State U. needs business people like Cliff, and Cliff needs me. The Board is just now learning how to be fiscally responsible, you know, like the big corporations. One way we've become more fiscally responsible is by having two sets of accounting books — a real one that nobody gets to see and another one that we release to the public when a newspaper or some big organization files a freedom of information lawsuit.

Ivy Tower to Wall Street

To make the ivy tower to Wall Street transition, we're dumping foolishly idealistic professors as campus leaders. They're a bunch of liberals, anyhow. Cliff calls them geeks and whackos. Meetings with them are awful. They talk all day and can never make up their minds about anything. They're so boring. That's why we're getting rid of them. Governing boards don't need whackos. We need experienced lawyers (better than the ones we have now, for sure) and businessmen (well, some of them can be women). Of course, nobody likes lawyers (except for Matlock on TV reruns), but we still need lawyers. After all, who else but a lawyer knows how to screw people over left and right and get away with it?

The rest of us on the board are business people. Business people know why kids need college degrees. To get good jobs. That's why. So what if you just slip by. No big deal. You can still get a great job. Look at me and Cliff. Our jobs are great. Lawyers and business-type people, like me and Cliff, know how to run university governing boards and administrative offices. Our Board is not into education, but we know business. We're real litigious (meaning we fight every grievance and legal case to the death—just like corporations) and we're real business-like (meaning we cater to the economic needs of the state's corporations).

Putting Professors in their Places

One of the jobs we have on the Board is to review promotion packets of professors. Each time a professor wants to be promoted, he or she must turn in a bunch of papers called a promotion packet. Professors get huge salary increases each time they get promoted, so they're all the time turning in packets. Reviewing professors' packets could take us a real long time if we read any of the stuff they shove into their promotion packets. But we don't read any of it. This is because the professors write way too much and they exaggerate everything. Cliff says, "They don't exaggerate! They make everything up! It's all a bunch of B.S."

I figure, if the professors make everything up, like Cliff says, why bother reading their packets. That's just stupid. Besides, the president knows about each professor, especially the troublemakers. So he knows how we should vote. We just do what he says. It's easier that way.

The president tells us which professors are troublemakers and which ones are O.K. to promote. He has a list of troublemakers. This way we know to vote against the troublemakers. Everybody else gets promoted. That's how the system works. But there are some procedures to follow. One procedure is to take packets home over the weekend and then to bring them back on Monday. Each round of promotion, the president gives us a few packets to take home over the weekend. He knows we won't read them, so he doesn't even ask. But the procedures say he has to give us packets and the procedures say we have to take them home.

There are hundreds of pages of procedures in the State U. contract with the faculty. Well, Cliff says hundreds, but I never looked at the contract. None of us on the Board pays any attention to all those procedure pages. We just take the packets home over the weekend like the president tells us. When the president gives me promotion packets, I haul them down to my den along with a cooler full of six packs (I always buy a brand of beer that comes in red and gold cans—to match the colors of my den). I pile the packets up in front of my 60-inch projection TV. Then I prop my feet on the pile of packets (they make a real good foot rest) and I watch NFL games all weekend. If there's no football game on, I just switch to hockey or wrestling. Sunday night, when the last game is over, and the six packs are killed, I dust off the top packet (it's got all that shoe crud on it). Monday morning I take the packets back to the president's office on my way to work (Fig. 20.1).

One time last year, I looked at a packet. (The game I was watching wasn't that good, anyhow.) Attached to the inside cover of the packet was a little Post-It note from the president with the word "TROUBLEMAKER" in bold red letters. That got me interested, so I read a bit of the packet. And you know what? It was just like Cliff had said. The packet was a bunch of made-up stuff. This professor hadn't been promoted in eighteen years. Right off, I know he was no good. He claimed to have raised $800,000 in teaching biotechnology short courses to industrial scientists. Nonsense! Nobody can make that kind of money teaching. Maybe a thousand dollars, but never $800,000. I mean, that's more than I make at Amalgamated and I'm not even a teacher—I work for a living. He said he trained eighty-four undergraduate research students in his own laboratory. What does he think? We're stupid or something. Nobody works that hard—certainly not a professor.

But wait, there's more. He said he had run three huge international symposia in a cutting-edge research area with 1000 registrants (or some ridiculously high number) and, get this, he said he did all the planning and all the administration by himself. What a crock! How could he possibly do all this by himself? He probably had twenty or thirty other professors and scads of secretaries helping him out. No professor in State U. history has ever run

Hey Doc! Does Speling Count?

(Fig. 20.1)

three huge international symposia alone. This guy had to be lying through his teeth. And then, just to grab all the credit, he left out the names of the people who did the real work. What a sleaze

The B.S. continues. He said that he had several important patents. Then he said he had the heaviest teaching load in the department plus an international reputation in one of the hottest areas of biotechnology research. He said he was invited to give keynote research talks at all sorts of international meetings and that he was an author of the most quoted paper in his field. Come on! Are you an overworked teacher or a famous researcher?

Don't try to convince us you're both. We weren't born yesterday, Mr. Important World-Famous Professor! But there's still more. He claimed to have a few thousand citations in the scientific literature, a bunch of book chapters, lots of journal articles, and thirty-one papers at international meetings. Could this guy ever pour it on! The president has ordered us never to approve promotion applications from this professor. So we turned him down flat. That should shut him up real good.

Other Ways We Silence the Professors

Not everything is perfect at State U. Like, we have problems with technology transfer. Well, the problem is not really with tech transfer. The problem is with the professors. Do you know about technology transfer? Probably not. Technology transfer is about being sure the university keeps all the money when a professor invents something. Professors are always inventing something or other and they want to keep all the royalty money for themselves. You'd think we didn't give them great salaries and all. Most of the professor's inventions are junk. No way they'll make money for the university by inventing junk. So tech transfer has to sort out the good inventions from the bad ones. Sorting out inventions is real hard work because every professor thinks his stupid invention is the greatest.

We even have a professor at State U. who invented a new kind of toothpick by folding a little piece of paper in half. He had technical drawings and everything. What a dumb idea! It took tech transfer years to get him off their backs. He was so pushy. State U. has a great bunch of tech transfer folks. They're real sharp and they never stop working, it seems. But they can't manage to get anything done because they have to work with those pushy, stuck-up professors.

Wait until you get to know a few professors personally. You'll find out how pushy and stuck-up professors are. Professors are in their own little worlds. Nobody can work with them. Not students, not deans, not tech transfer people, and certainly not the president of State U. He's always telling the Board how impossible it is to work with the State U. faculty. I believe him. Professors don't even like football and basketball. They just like putting crazy liberal ideas into student's heads and writing books and things nobody reads.

It's not just books professors write. They write crazy letters and emails to the president, the State U. Board, and even the governor's office. Professors are totally out of it, so we never pay attention to what they write. Every month we pass their crazy letters around the table in our private Board meeting, just to get a good laugh. That's the best part of being on the Board—laughing at professors' letters. After lunch, we throw those crazy letters away. The president has a policy that nobody in the administration is allowed to answer any professor's letter. The president doesn't, so we never do either. Just like the president, we ignore all the letters. Cliff wrote this policy all by himself. It's a real good piece of writing. Plus, it gives us a whole lot less work to do. Here's one letter that came to us from a whacko professor a few months ago. Adhering to the president's policy, nobody ever answered it. But the letter was so dumb, I saved it for this book. Here it is:

Dear President L-------,

I write this letter to make you aware of a growing problem in the State U. office of Technology Transfer. My concern is that this office does little or no technology transfer and little or no corporate liaison. I am not sure what they do, but they provide very few useful services to the entrepreneurial faculty.

When professors develop new technology, the technology transfer office seems unable to promote the technology. They don't effectively present professors inventions to potential licensees. It's almost as if no one in tech transfer reads the description of an invention before filing it away.

Out of sheer frustration with this ineffective tech transfer bureaucracy, professors turn over inventions to corporations for free. As a result, corporations acquire university-generated technology and intellectual property for nothing. The university technology transfer administrators seem unable to reverse this trend.

Despite these problems, I believe there are reasonable ways to advance our common goals. I would be more than pleased to partner with the administration in finding ways for technology transfer officials and faculty entrepreneurs to work more effectively with each other. Please let me know your thoughts.

    Sincerely,

    Professor W---

When we passed this letter around, Cliff laughed so much he choked on the filet mignon they served us for lunch. Lucky I was nearby with a big glass of Dom Perignon. He quick washed down the food with a big gulp of wine.

Then he finished the bottle. Cliff drinks a lot of wine at Board meetings. I mean a lot! I saw him drink five whole bottles at a Board meeting luncheon one time. Usually it's only three.

Magnetic Neucular Residents Machines

Another thing that professors keep fussing about is how we spend money at State U. They act like they should have a say in how money is spent. No corporation works this way. The CEO makes the decisions on spending money—no questions asked. At State U., the president makes the money decisions, not the professors. Still, professors want more money for classroom teaching, like labs and things. They want crumby old teaching buildings fixed up real fancy like. A lot of old buildings at State U. aren't worth fixing. No sense spending good money on real old buildings. They're just used for teaching and stuff, anyhow. So who cares?

Professors are never happy with old buildings. They keep complaining about toilets that won't flush, windows that won't open or close, sinks that won't drain, lights that don't work, and doors that won't lock. They fuss about flooded labs, broken desks, crumbling staircases, and broken air conditioners. They fuss when overhead sewer pipes leak on their precious books and manuscripts. There is no end to their complaining.

A while back, we even got a letter about squeaky chalk from some picky professor. We just passed this letter around at a Board meeting and laughed. Professors want every student to have a place to sit in lecture classes and some even want as much as $500 a year for supplies and equipment to teach 100 students in chemistry lab classes. Hey! That's seven dollars per student. We can't afford this kind of money. Why can't professors buy stuff at Wal-Mart, like everybody else?

At State U. we save our money for important new projects like brand new research centers for SuperCola and top-of-the-line weight rooms so we can get better at football. No sense wasting good money on those teaching professors and all their demands for non-squeaky chalk. Hey! If the squeaky kind is cheaper, we go for it. That's just good business. We won't spend money on teaching professors. Not when we have other professors who do free testing for big corporations with government grants from the NFS, or whatever it's called. So we put up whole new buildings for these professors so they can keep getting their NFS money, MOLDY-TOV's and Magnetic Neucular Residents machines.

Does SuperCola Taste Better?

Some people don't understand how this money thing works at State U. I was very confused at first until Cliff explained it all to me. Actually, it's real simple. State U. gets lots of money from the state. That's why it's called State U. instead of just plain U. The state legislators who pass money bills are all lawyers and businessmen (well, some are women). Just like in business, they want their State U. investments to bring in money.

Like, if a guy in the state assembly is a director of SuperCola, he wants State U. to sell only SuperCola on campus. So, if the president agrees to throw out all the other campus vendors, this SuperCola guy will write a real big State U. appropriations bill. In return, he may want a huge, expensive new research center at State U. to test whether SuperCola tastes better than the other colas. This testing takes big fancy machines like MNR machines, CL mess spectrometers, MOLDY-TOV's, HPLE, and such (see Chapter 19). By the way, HPLE is short for High Pressure Liquid Encephalograph. HPLE's are real important—just like MOLDY-TOV's and MNR machines. All these machines are run by computers, so that just shows you how important they are for our centers.

A while back, when we were working on plans for a SuperCola Institute at State U., SuperCola made us a great deal. They gave us 1500 ten-year-old PC's they valued at $10 million. All we had to do was give SuperCola a monopoly on concessions at State U. That was easy. So we did it. Now we have $10 million worth of computers and computer parts piled one on top of another at Surplus Properties. The student newspaper made a federal case out of the computers being ten years old. They said the computers are totally worthless. I bet no student yanked a SuperCola computer from under the pile at Surplus Properties to see if it works. Am I right or what?

Students also complained about our playing the SuperCola jingle at basketball and football games. Frankly, we're sick of the student newspaper. It's not up to them to manage State U. The president does this. So if the editors fuss again, we'll just shut down their silly newspaper for good. And they know it. So those liberal student newspaper people better put a lid on it. We call this checks and balances. We pay the checks and they balance the news coverage—the way we like it. They should just write stories about how state corporations benefit from our high-tech centers.

State U. has about 100 high-tech centers doing all kinds of testing for big corporations. This is real good for the state's economy because the big corporations don't have to pay for the MOLDY-TOV's and Magnetic

Neucular Residents themselves. They get State U. to buy them with taxpayer money. Our main job on the State U. board is working out all these deals with big corporations and building lots of new centers to do the testing for the corporations. Our State U. centers work real cheap because taxpayers foot the bills.

First, people pay taxes to the state government. Then the state government gives money to State U. so we can buy MOLDY-TOV's and stuff and pay the salaries of the professors. The professors do work for the big corporations, saving them tons of money. Cliff worked real hard on this system and now it practically runs itself. Cliff is great at this stuff. He does a whole year's planning in a couple of days. This way he can spend most of his time on football and basketball.

Oh, yeah! Cliff wants me to tell you he bought thirty-six extra MOLDY-TOV's by mistake. Each one cost $680,000, but we're selling them at a ten percent discount. If you want one, just email us at cheapmoldytovs@stateu.edu. We'll even kick in the postage for free.

WWF and University Management

The newest kids on the university block are nouveau riche executives from the World Wrestling Federation (WWF). These WWF guys are popping up left and right within university administrations. We've got two on the State U. Board already. They have the required credentials to participate fully in university management. They are real wealthy and they're politically connected--especially in Minnesota. And they're totally into sports. They blend in well with the rest of us on the board.

WWF executives were invited into academic management for their ability to make scads of money. The president hopes they will do for State U. what they have done for professional wrestling. He says the WWF guys are nothing short of financial wizards. In less than a decade they've transformed a moribund, lifeless, and penniless alleged sport (professional wrestling) into a profit-making circus that captures the heart and soul of America's male youth. Boys, from pre-toddlers to mid-teens, are captivated and transfixed by the WWF spectacles on their private bedroom TVs. The Federation has had its ups and downs with the XFL (the X-rated football league) but they've learned from their mistakes. The XFL should have been placed on college campuses where good sex is appreciated.

Butt-Naked Cheerleaders

The grand campus plan of the WWF is to transform state university athletics as they have transformed big-time professional sports. The WWF is currently planning a huge university alliance called the XSUL (pronounced just as written). This will be an X-rated sports league of state universities. A high-level WWF delegation has been to talk with our own Board. Their plan sounds great! The mission of the XSUL will be to place university sports into sort of a professional league controlled by the WWF. As with professional wrestling, entertainment will be the key. The biggest part of the package will be a new form of college football. College football will become bigger, bolder, and more brazen under the XSUL umbrella. No expense will be spared. A particularly attractive feature of the XSUL plan is butt-naked college cheerleaders. Cliff's eyes almost popped out of his head when the WWF guys told us this. Butt-naked cheerleaders! Wow! What an idea.

Butt-naked cheerleaders are expected to increase local attendance and television revenues for just about every college team in the country. Imagine the binocular sales! Souvenir State U. binocular sales could become a multi-million dollar concession. Me and Cliff see a bonanza when Amalgamated gets this contract. Big guns from the WWF expect the XSUL football plan to burst (or should that be "bust"?) onto the scene in a year or two. The dollars are in place. All the leading men's magazines have sunk millions into the project, just for the photography rights. State university presidents are falling in line like bunnies.

For several years, key university presidents and governing boards across the country have been slaving away on the XSUL plan. Until recently, they have been hampered by backwards management teams full of professors. Professors have no imagination. But things are changing. We're getting rid of the professors. As we phase out professors, we recruit WWF executives to join university governing boards. The new boards are able to move rapidly toward the XSUL vision. Cliff is out in front on this one. (Somebody told me this is a pun. I don't get it). Cliff's plans are listed in Table 20.1. They include the XSUL and much more.

TABLE 20.1:
CLIFF'S PLANS FOR THE XSUL REVOLUTION

---

1. Eliminate tenure and then dump old-fashioned faculty.
2. Hire new multi-talented faculty with experience in the entertainment industry.
3. Lower academic standards to accommodate future students.
4. Revamp the university management team by hiring university presidents and senior officers from the sports business sector.
5. Greatly increase the size of in-house legal teams. Get much better lawyers than the jerks we have now.
6. Turn over major management decisions to autonomous lawyers and experts in public relations, marketing, and finance.
7. Raise tuition.
8. Create new centers by marrying academic programs with appropriately self-interested corporations. As an inducement, let the corporations direct what is taught in classes and how material is to be presented. Lucrative corporate-academic partnerships might include: The Allied Chemical School of Environmental Remediation; The Andersen Center for Creative Accounting; The Heritage Foundation Center for Enlightened, Progressive Political Thought; and The Dr. Laura School of Secular Pop Psychobabble. Other possibilities include: The R. J. Reynolds School for Prevention of Respiratory Disorders; The Seagrams Seven Center for the Study of Substance Abuse; The Rush Limbaugh School of Humble, Modest, and Unbiased Political Polling; The Enron School for Regulation of Corporate Ethics; The Penthouse Institute for the Prevention of Sexual Exploitation; and The National Rifle Association Center for the Proliferation of Domestic Gun Violence.
9. Affiliate with a major importer of high quality binoculars. What a gold mine for Amalgamated Importers!

The emergence of the XSUL presents bold, new opportunities for high school students—college life that is totally fun. Students will be quick to discover which universities are joining the XSUL and they will want to be part of the action. They'll all want to select a college or university in the thick of the XSUL revolution. If this interests you, better get your application in fast. The competition will be fierce. No one can afford to delay.

You might want to buy your binoculars before you leave for college. You'll want a real good pair to view the real good pairs on the football field. More than anything, everybody wants a clear image. Shop around in your hometown. Amalgamated Importers will soon be providing official State U. binoculars to hometown shops and department stores around the state. Amalgamated binoculars won't be cheap, but they'll have that great Bulldogs emblem glued to the side. Nobody can resist a souvenir that displays the likeness of a great college football mascot, like the State U. Bulldog.

CHAPTER 21

HOW UNIVERSITIES GOVERN THEMSELVES

The Oligarchical Democracy

There are three ways to govern organizations, or so it has been said: (1) the right way, (2) the wrong way, and (3) the military way. People who believe this don't know much about university governance. Universities are unique. Cliff says universities govern themselves by combining the wrong way with the military way to come up with a system he calls the oligarchical democracy. Cliff explains the oligarchical democracy as a hybrid system of governance in which all power rests with a small autonomous group of people (the oligarchy part). The democracy portion of the system is totally controlled by the oligarchy part (see "The PPBR Panel" subheading to follow). At State U., the oligarchy is the university president and a handful of his chosen yes-persons (YP's). Cliff is trying to get promoted to YP in the president's cabinet. But he's not there yet. Cliff knows so much stuff. It's a shame the president hasn't chosen him. You see, as regular Board members, me and Cliff have no authority. The president makes all the decisions. He's like a dictator. We just rubber-stamp everything he says.

Figure 21.1 shows the official State U. organizational chart. It sort of puts everything into perspective. Now, let me tell you about how the Governing Board does business.

What Goes On at State U. Board Meetings

The State U. Governing Board meets one day each month. First there's the private luncheon meeting of the Board along with the president and his yes-person cabinet. The president begins the meeting by passing around recent letters from the professors. He likes to start meetings off on a jocular note (come on Cliff, what does this mean?). Then, after we all get a few belly laughs, he throws the letters away. Next he presents the agenda and tells us how to vote on each item in the afternoon public meeting to follow. Presentation of the agenda takes only a few minutes—the president does all the talking. We always vote exactly as he tells us, so what's to discuss. Then comes lunch. The meals are unbelievable. Lunch must cost $10,000 for just eleven Board members. The State U. Board is the best country club I've ever seen. And it's all for free! Laughable letters and lavish lunches are the two best parts of State U. Board meetings.

After lunch, the Board meets publicly with the visitors where we approve everything on the president's agenda without discussion. We couldn't talk if we wanted—not with all the expensive, imported wine we had at lunch. Even when sober, we discuss nothing in public meetings because we all want to stay on the Board. Visitors, like professors, students, and such, are allowed to attend Board meetings, but the president picks a real long narrow room to keep visitors as far away from him as possible. The president orders guards to put up rope barriers like they have at the movies. That keeps visitors about 200 yards away from the president. He's scared of visitors. He got elbowed by one a long time ago. Visitors get a chance to talk for about three minutes, but only if their written comments have been pre-approved by the president. We don't have to listen to any of the visitors because the president already told us how to vote on every agenda item when we had our private meeting before lunch. Cliff says we have to meet with the visitors because of some law—moonshine law or something, I think he called it.

The PPBR Panel

To keep up the appearance of democracy, the president of State U. needs lots of committees. He selects committee members by himself. State U. committees are a bit different from those in most organizations. In most

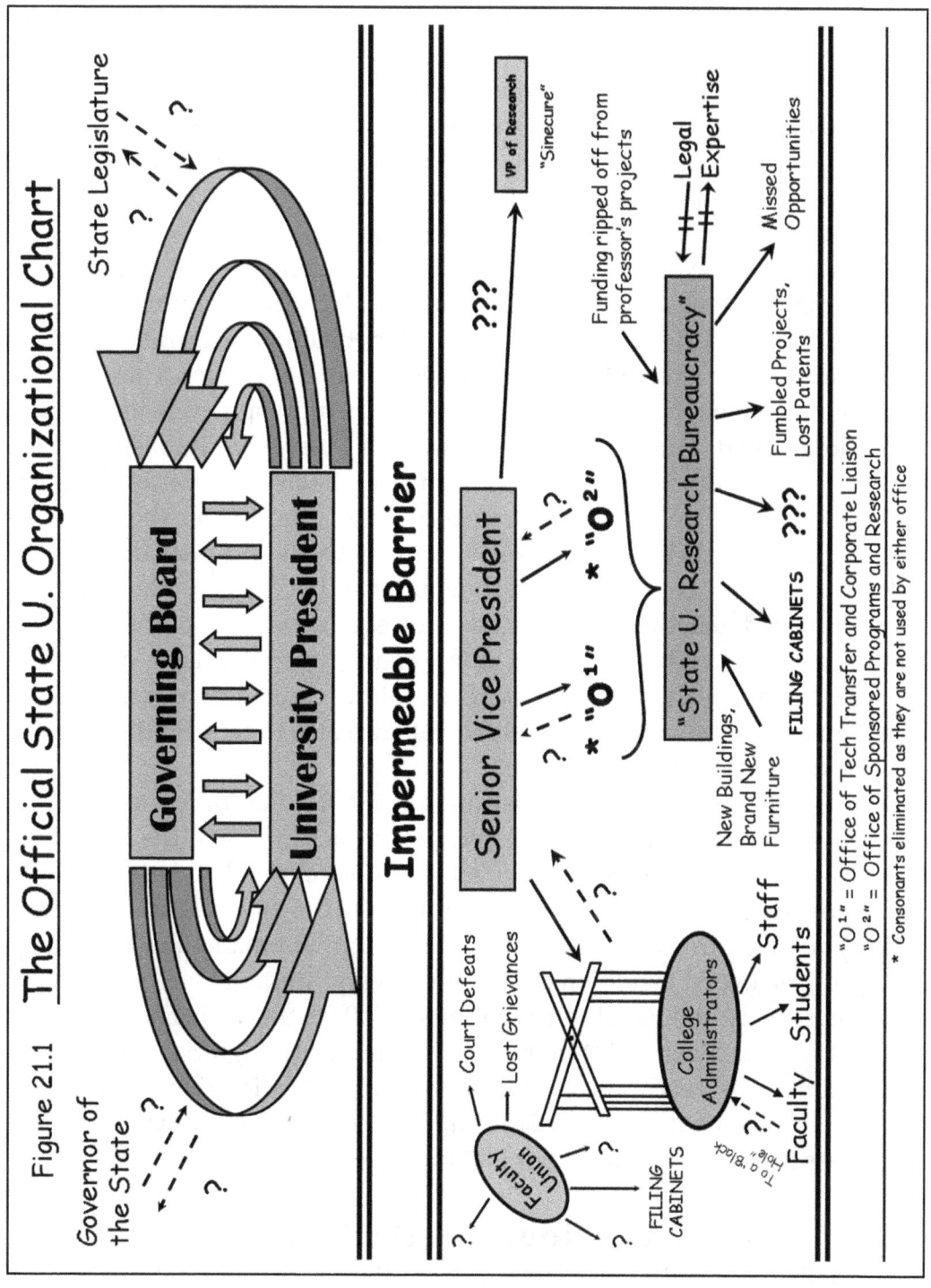

Figure 21.1 The Official State U. Organizational Chart

organizations, committees make independent recommendations. But at State U. the president requires each committee member to vote in favor of his positions. The president also invites students to serve on these committees, but nobody ever pays attention to students.

All State U. committees stem from a single administration-appointed group known as the President's Permanent Blue Ribbon Panel (the PPBR Panel). Members of the PPBR Panel include students, faculty, and administrators. At one Board meeting, the president told us how he picks PPBR members. Here's what the president said. He talks real pompous.

"I pick each PPBR Panelist carefully and meticulously. Each Panelist must have world-class credentials, an impeccable reputation, and instant international name recognition. Each must be the undisputed leader of his or her academic field. Panelists in the liberal arts must have published at least 250,000 pages worth of critically acclaimed scholarly books and refereed publications. (Refereed means somebody read the paper before it got published). A Panelist from the sciences must be the original discoverer of matter (or at least cadmium, molybdenum, and feldspar). He must have several hundred generally accepted laws or equations (and perhaps a planet or two) named after him or her. I don't count Murphy's Law or the Peter Principle. I strongly encourage Nobel Prizes. But I don't accept just any Nobel Prize winner. I personally review all Nobel laureates to be sure they meet the rigorous standards of State U.

"All Panelists from the administration must have accumulated academic credentials comparable to those listed for faculty panelists. Obviously university administrators will have achieved at or above this level or they would not have gotten to be administrators in the first place. In addition, Panel appointees from the administration must command the respect and admiration of every faculty member and every student. I require student representatives on the Panel to have scored 1600 on the SAT. Each must have appeared on the cover of "Who's Who in American High Schools" for four years running and each must have been class valedictorian of his or her respective high school. Each student I appoint to the Panel must be a former senior class president and a former National Merit Scholarship winner."

Back-Door Routes to the PPBR Panel

Cliff tells the PPBR story different from the president. Real different! He says candidates for the President's Permanent Blue Ribbon Panel often fall short of the president's stated criteria. These less notable individuals, says

Cliff, are still eligible to become Panelists. Such candidates must meet two alternate criteria. First, they must be willing to accept, with grace and without question, the totally concocted, fabricated, and misleading accolades the university president manufactures for each Panelist. Second, they must vote with the president on every issue, expressing unwavering support for the administration position.

Rumors persist that some appointees to the President's Permanent Blue Ribbon Panel sneak in through the back door. The fact of the matter, says Cliff, is that every Panelist enters by the back door. Each is a flat-out dufus and an unabashed administration lackey. Most have no academic credentials at all. I think one professor on the State U. PPBR Panel published a poem about twenty years ago. Another had a brief story in Colliers Magazine a while back. While these dufus-lackeys have no academic careers and no reputations outside of State U., the president puts them on just about every State U. committee. They're so busy going from one committee meeting to another, they barely have time to teach one lecture a year if the TA gets sick or something. It's the same with student members of the PPBR Panel — meeting after meeting after meeting. But, since nobody ever pays attention to the students, they can use that committee time to write test answers on their hands and arm casts.

Students on the PPBR Panel are no more qualified than the professors. A student who scored only 811 on the SAT and ranked 249th in his or her graduating class of 250 is a shoe-in for the President's Permanent Blue Ribbon Panel. As with the chosen professors, a student must be willing to accept distorted personal accolades and be willing to bend to authority with 100 percent predictability.

Cliff says one of my new Board jobs is to recommend students for the PPBR Panel. Here's what Cliff says to do. Pick any beginning freshman at random. The student, having found his or her classroom buildings (this takes several weeks), should send a letter to the president volunteering to serve on the Panel. Table 21.1 shows such a letter. Cliff recommended this student and the president accepted him gladly. He's been on the PPBR panel for three years now. We currently use his letter as a model for other students to follow — it's one of the best letters we've gotten.

TABLE 21.1:
A GOOD STUDENT LETTER AS APPLICATION FOR THE UNIVERSITY PRESIDENT'S PERMANENT BLUE RIBBON PANEL

> Dear President L-------,
> I just learned about your blue panel thing and I want to be on it. I'm not what you call a real good student and all, but I did get a C+ in plane geometry when I took it a second time. I don't know why they call it plane geometry. We didn't do nothing about airplanes all year. Also, I was vice-president of my fifth grade class (Mrs. Dixon's room), so I know about being a leader and stuff. Oh, yeah. I almost forgot. I play offensive tackle on the football team. Being I weigh 373 pounds is real helpful. I'm a Republican, a born-again evangelist, a right-to-lifer, and a member of the NRA. I've been in army ROTC since ninth grade, and my father is the leader of an all-white, all-male paramilitary cult in Eastern Oregon. So I'm real good at taking orders and I don't never ask any questions. How do I sign up for the blue panel thing?
>
> Very Respectively Yours,
>
> (Your name goes here)

Ignore the President's Boondoggles

So, according to Cliff, every student I recommend is sure to get selected under the alternate criteria. The president needs lots of students and faculty on his Permanent Blue Ribbon Panel. He has to pretend that talented students and world-class faculty are actually involved in university-wide decisions. He has to play democracy games. He's afraid of the consequences if he doesn't. If people found out he's a dictator, there could be uprisings and revolts. There could be sit-ins and protest marches and State U. pennant burnings conducted by the deans and lesser assistant administrators, in solidarity with students and faculty. There could be armed police in riot gear surrounding the president's mansion and spraying mace and pepper spray all over his prize petunias and geraniums. There could be National Guardsmen with rifles and flack suits storming the president's office and occupying the building until he relinquishes control of the university. Filling the airways could be countless military helicopters, each with an officer leaning out an open window and shouting obscenities at the president through a giant bullhorn. This is what the president of State U. fears if people learn he's a dictator. This is why he is obsessed with playing democracy games.

While he tries to disguise his true identity with democracy games, the president is a control freak. There is no democracy at State U. Being on the President's Permanent Blue Ribbon Panel is, therefore, pointless. The Panel and its democracy games are a farce and every Panelist knows it. But students have a blast serving on presidential committees. They get real good food too. Cliff keeps telling me students can remain on the PPBR Panel only by keeping silent. The instant a Panelist offers the slightest opposition to a single boondoggle idea of the president, he's out the door. So if you get on the Panel, don't forget to keep your mouth shut at meetings. Don't even think about uttering a word.

Type I and Type II Problems

As you recall from Chapter 5, two types of problems reach the desks of university presidents. These are referred to as Type I and Type II problems. Type I problems are those brought to the president by concerned students, faculty, and staff (like the 388 requests for a sign for Barnaby Hall—see Chapter 5). University presidents never attempt solution of Type I problems, just as a matter of policy. This is because Type I problems originate outside the realm of administration. Administrators define such problems as unimportant and beneath their dignity. Sometimes Type I problems indict members of the administration for gross mismanagement. Sometimes they indict the president himself. Sometimes criminal mischief comes to the fore. Sometimes the mischief is felonious. So Type I problems are instantly deep-sixed, never to surface again. Cliff thinks the State U. president is dumb not to do anything about Type I problems. Not addressing the Type I's just makes the faculty mad as hornets. In fact, Cliff says the State U. president is just dumb in general. So, anyway, back to the Type I's. Cliff put together Table 21.2. It's got a few Type I problems the State U. president has ignored in the past twelve years.

TABLE 21.2:
REAL TYPE I PROBLEMS IGNORED OR KILLED BY THE STATE U. PRESIDENT

1. More than half the students registered for NASDAQ Stock Tips are sitting in the aisles and exits, as all seats are full. Faculty and student complaints are ignored by the administration.

2. A dean unilaterally demolishes a teaching laboratory, displacing ten laboratory classes without considering where those classes will now have to meet. The demolished lab remains vacant for years while displaced faculty scramble for temporary facilities. A professor's million-dollar outreach program is nearly destroyed by this huge disruption. When finally renovated and re-occupied, the space is greatly under-utilized by its new occupant—some guy who's into smelly old landfills and wierd shrubs, I think.

3. New construction on campus presents a serious health and safety risk, as nearby pedestrian paths are destroyed. For months, students and faculty are forced to walk on slippery, muddy, irregular paths alongside moving vehicles. Appeals to State U. health and safety officials are ignored. Several students and faculty members are injured by passing cars. Still there's no administration response. Nothing happens, in fact, until a huge faculty outcry forces a nine-member team of administrators to do a site visit. Only because one of the administrators in high heels refuses to walk on the same muddy paths traveled for two years by faculty and students is anything done to make the walkway safe. It helped that a professor was there with a camera to record the high-heeled administrator's refusal to "walk the walk."

4. A student's major is suddenly abolished in her senior year and she must transfer to another department. Her transfer to an alternate major forces her to stay an additional year.

(For more of Cliff's examples of Type I problems see Appendix.)

Before Type I problems reach the president's desk, just to be ignored or suppressed, dozens of lesser assistant administrators, under presidential orders, pass the problems around from desk to desk for several years. According to Cliff, while they're passing Type I problems around, the lesser assistant administrators follow the following unpublished guidelines:

1. Never assume responsibility for a Type I problem if it can be passed to another lesser assistant administrator. If possible, pass the buck to one who has recently transferred to another department or to one who has been demoted to the position of lower, lesser assistant administrator. Better yet, pass the Type I along to someone who died around the turn of the century—the 19th century, that is.
2. Never identify the lower, lesser assistant administrator to whom you have passed the buck. Affected students, faculty, or staff persons must never learn who's holding the buck. If they learn the identity of the "buck holder," they might pressure him or her to work on a solution to the problem. Then you'll get all the flack for letting the "cat out of the bag." Most importantly, don't let the president know who is handling the issue. One little mistake and the president will trash the poor slob.
3. Never let anyone know you've have assumed the slightest personal responsibility for a Type I, even if the buck should land squarely on your desk. No need to put your neck on the chopping block.
4. Never let someone else do the work for you. By delegating responsibility or by sharing responsibility with others, you may demonstrate your own uselessness.
5. Never do the work yourself. Helping to solve Type I problems is not your responsibility.
6. Establish a paper trail allowing the president to crush troublemakers any time he wishes.
7. Never miss lunch.

ESQ People

The State U. president delays the solutions of all Type I problems indefinitely. Never is a Type I problem resolved! If the president is sufficiently patient, Type I problems will simply vanish, usually upon the demise of the person who raised the issue. However, dozens of university lawyers may be required to delay a case for ten, twenty, or thirty years. Cliff doesn't like the president and he hates his cabal of lackey-lawyers, big time. He calls them ESQ People on account of the ESQ abbreviation they stick after their names. ESQ is short for the Latin word "esquirmae," meaning sneaky, slimy, or salamanderish (and my boss at Amalgamated Importers said I'd never have an occasion to use my high school Latin—that shows how little he knows). According to Cliff, there aren't always enough ESQ People to satisfy the president. As more Type I cases come up, more ESQ People are needed. The president wants these cases delayed at any cost. Sometimes the president raises tuition just to add more ESQ People to the payroll. It's expensive to hire ESQ People whose sole function is to delay cases. While they are quite willing to act immorally, ESQ People charge higher fees and retainers than legitimate lawyers (Cliff says "legitimate lawyers" is the best oxymoron he has ever seen—remember, Cliff, "legitimate lawyers" is my joke, not yours).

But university presidents are able to hire as many ESQ People as they want. After all, the president controls income and expenses without meaningful oversight. Hey, it doesn't matter one hoot what me and Cliff say in Board meetings. The president does whatever he pleases, including hiring ESQ People. Generally, State U. has hundreds of ESQ People handling hundreds of cases, each in a permanent delay pattern. If there are enough university ESQ People working on a particular case, that case can be delayed until all the interested parties (students, faculty, or staff) graduate, retire, or kick the bucket. This is the game plan. It works well. Cliff explained Type I problems to me over a couple of beers at our favorite pub. Then he switched to Type II problems.

Cliff says that Type II problems are entirely different. These are problems originating solely within the administration. Type II problems are addressed immediately and, if at all possible, solved on the spot. Table 21.3 lists some representative Type II problems:

TABLE 21.3:
SOME TYPICAL TYPE II PROBLEMS

1. The president desires a 20-percent salary raise
2. The president wishes to recruit the most expensive football coach in the history of the game.
3. The president wishes to raise tuition seventeen percent to pay for the new football coach ($975,000 per year base pay for seven years with fourteen percent guaranteed annual increase in base salary plus $285,000 incentive for each football victory).
4. The president wants to stick State U. with making multimillion-dollar severance pay for two complete coaching staffs he fired, unilaterally last year.
5. The president needs thirty-seven more in-house ESQ People to handle a single litigation case directed at him, personally.
6. The president needs to reward a loyal member of the Governing Board by pushing in his direction a huge university contract.
7. The president wishes to detenure (fire) a professor who has exercised freedom of speech by expressing criticism of the president's administration.
8. The president makes a Trent Lott-type racial gaffe that creates an international stir. He demands that State U. employ a racially balanced entourage of professional actors to follow him around for photo-ops until the thing settles down. In particular, he wants that what's-his-name, sanctimonious NRA spokes-model actor to follow him in public in blackface.

According to Cliff, Type II problems need immediate attention, as they originate from the president and his administration. The president demands that Type II problems be solved on the spot. Upper level administrators usually rally together to solve Type II problems on the same day they come up. If the solution to a particularly sensitive Type II problem could possibly see the light of day, the president mobilizes the President's Permanent Blue Ribbon Panel to cover his tracks.

Cliff orders a couple more drafts (he likes those 36-ounce glasses, nearly the size of a football) and then he explains how the President's Permanent

Blue Ribbon Panel was mobilized to solve a Type II problem—one that came up before I got on the State U. Board. The problem was how to get better computers and computer systems for the top-level administrators. This Type II was all the president's idea. Cliff didn't like the plan from the start. He says the administrators had gotten new computers just ten months earlier, plus we still had that huge pile of SuperCola rejects over in Surplus Properties. So getting new computers now was a huge waste of money. But there wasn't a damn thing Cliff could do about the plan. It was driven by the president and by his YP's. Cliff kept drinking and talking until the bar closed. He was really upset about how State U. got new computers for the administration and he told me just how it happened.

It started when the State U. president attended a Sunday afternoon cocktail party with presidents of other universities. One of the other presidents told him that State U. is years behind other colleges and universities with respect to on-campus computer networking for administrators and researchers. This was just a real big joke, but, hey, it was a cocktail party and the other guys were just having fun with State U. Probably on account of we lose every football game. Our president thinks it's for real. He's not too smart, if you remember. So, our not-too-smart State U. president makes an impulsive, unilateral, and irreversible decision. After the seventh Martini, he decides that State U. needs to revamp computer facilities for its administrators.

Monday morning, between doses of Alka Seltzer and still a little weak at the knees, he consults with his cabinet of YP's about implementing his new computer plan. Normally Board members wouldn't learn such intimate details of presidential deliberations, but Cliff is a bar-hopping buddy of one of the president's YP's. The YP tells Cliff what happened Monday morning. At that meeting, the YP's indicate that the state legislature is not in the mood for such a plan. Just like me and Cliff, most of the legislators have little respect for the president of State U. They would never fund a computer upgrade for administrators so long as this guy is running State U. The YP's tell the president that the computers-for-administrators plan must be packaged as a computers-for-students plan. The president accepts this strategy and mobilizes his "democracy network" to push the plan through.

So the president selects, from the PPBR panel, a blue ribbon committee to study the need for student computer facilities. Cliff's own student nominee gets selected. You know. The 373-pound offensive lineman who thought plane geometry was about aviation and learned leadership skills in Mrs.

Dixon's fifth grade class. That's the one. It's fun for students to get on blue ribbon committees. The administrators treat them real good and they're not required to go to meetings where votes are cast. Not bad! The president designates the blue ribbon committee as a university-wide Students' Information Age Study Commission (SIASC). The president relies upon the long, unblemished voting record of PPBR Panelists. Committee members quickly realize the computer plan is not for students but for the administration. But they're willing to keep the secret and to package the plan as if it were for students. They know their roles. For this loyalty, SIASC appointees will breeze through promotion ahead of schedule and receive merit pay raises on every cycle. SIASC students will get the best recommendation letters to law school the president can concoct.

The fifty-seven in-house public relations officials and staff members, who report to the State U. Vice-President for Image and Perception (VPIP), create a promotional plan. This is dubbed the students' Computer Retrofitting And Procurement project. The acronym, CRAP, is a most unfortunate abbreviation. Apparently, the VPIP didn't foresee how the committee name would be abbreviated. Now EVERYBODY is laughing behind the president's back. The VPIP is very nervous.

Next, Cliff said, a high level meeting takes place between the VPIP and a powerful YP on the State U. Governing Board. This board member, Alvin, happens to be an executive for the computer software giant, MicroSmooth. Cliff has never liked Alvin, especially after he landed a huge university computer contract for MicroSmooth last year. Now Alvin's at it again. In cooperation with Alvin, the office of the VPIP creates a detailed CRAP plan. Within two weeks, the plan goes to SIASC for review.

SIASC members meet once over a lavish luncheon at a time when the student members are in class. Between the baked Alaska and the Frangelico, and with no prior discussion except "Please pass the caviar," they approve all aspects of CRAP by unanimous, unregistered voice vote. This is standard operating procedure. All president-appointed committees at State U. function this way. It's efficient. In public, the members of SIASC say how vital university committee service is. They talk about spending hundreds of hours in careful deliberation and debate and about reviewing thousands of pages of written materials. They'll say how attentive and responsive the president was throughout the process. What a bunch of bunk! You see, SIASC members all want more baked Alaska.

The V-P for Image and Perception (really pouring it on to make up for the

CRAP boondoggle) reports the following to the entire university community:

> During the past several months, at the direction of the President of State U., a university-wide commission of students, faculty, and administrators has been meeting regularly to consider the need to upgrade and modernize student computing facilities in classrooms, learning centers, and dormitory locations on each campus.
>
> This commission, the Students' Information Age Study Commission, SIASC, has met tirelessly throughout the semester to evaluate the current state of student computing facilities at State U. The committee invited sixteen outside computing experts from twelve major universities throughout the country to assist in evaluating State U.'s student computing facilities and projected needs. State U. is pleased to announce that this independent commission of dedicated State U. men and women recommends investing $26.3 million over the next five years for the modernization and upgrading of computer facilities for students on each campus of State U. They have produced a comprehensive, 137-page document called the '"Students' Computer Retrofitting And Procurement" plan. The plan was submitted to the President of State U. on September 14 for his consideration."

Note that the VPIP has now capitalized the S in "Students" to cover up the CRAP acronym. But the problem only gets worse. Opponents now chant at every meeting, "SCRAP CRAP! SCRAP CRAP! SCRAP CRAP!"

Now the President of State U. appoints an impartial, outside review team of three prominent administrators from other major universities to make a site visit and to review the SIASC document. Impartial? Bologna! They're all buddies of the State U. president who take turns approving each other's dumb ideas. The team, now designated the Presidential Review of Institutional Computer Capabilities, PRICC (another potentially embarrassing acronym), arrives for a two-day long stay. Weeks earlier, the VPIP sent each member of the three-person team a copy of the SIASC report. This way the PRICC's can approve everything in the SIASC document as soon as they arrive. Two days on campus is enough for five opulent meals with the President of State U. and his most trusted YP's, all of whom lobby the PRICC's to ratify the SIASC document. There are brief periods when large groups of faculty and large groups of students are permitted to meet with the PRICC's in scheduled group hearings, having submitted written questions in advance. A little time is available for answers to a few carefully screened questions. Then, with the aid of four members of the president's clerical staff, PRICC writes its report on day two, following a long exit interview with the president. PRICC endorses every point in the 137-page SIASC document with glowing praise.

The Office of the VPIP issues an immediate announcement of the PRICC report to the academic community and delivers a press release to all media outlets in the state. Then the office of the VPIP, armed with positive reports from SIASC, SCRAP, and PRICC, mounts a massive PR dog and pony show. VPIP representatives fan out over the campus, meeting with all faculty and student governing and consulting bodies. They work tirelessly to solicit ratification of the Student Computer Retrofitting And Procurement plan. They promise that all SCRAP funds will go for student computer upgrades. Not a penny will go for research or administration. What a bald-faced lie! But then, what's new for State U? In the end, students are told that they will face a one-time computer fee of $300 to raise $12 million to seed the SCRAP project. No significant opposition is registered and overwhelming ratification of SCRAP goes on the record.

Instantly, the State U. president rolls into place his stealth plans to hijack the $12 million paid by the students. He diverts every cent into computer upgrades for the administration. The diversion of funds never reaches the public. The outside auditing firm reveals nothing. Remember, they've been under exclusive contract with State U. for thirty years and know never to ask for the real set of books. The state matches the $12 million of seed money raised by the one-time "student computer fee."

Without consulting any group and without public disclosure, the State U. president converts the one-time computer fee of $300 into an annual student fee. This dictatorial act insures sufficient income for ongoing computer upgrades for administrators and for a variety of other administrative activities unrelated to the undergraduate teaching program. Finally, the president of State U. can get an Olympic-size indoor swimming pool installed in his mansion (Fig. 21.2). The computer assessment continues for years and years and no person or group that oversees State U. registers the slightest objection. No newspaper reporters even inquire. Why bother? It would take more than two hours of research to do a story on the SCRAP program. What reporter can spend more than two hours on a story? Better go with the fast-breaking story about the malfunctioning traffic light on College Avenue and how it's interfering with access to the homecoming parade.

Hey Doc! Does Speling Count?

(Fig. 21.2)

A year passes and unofficial reports indicate that eighty-five percent of the contracts granted under SCRAP go to MicroSmooth. Alvin gets his biggest payoff ever and Cliff is really pissed. Except for Cliff, no one cares or asks questions. The president of State U. pulls it off without a hitch. And he likes his new pool. He's getting up courage to try the 50-foot diving platform.

After everything is finished and the plan is fully implemented, me and Cliff are invited, along with the members of SIASC, to a grand reception and nine-course meal at the home of the university president. The spacious new patio adjoining his brand new indoor pool is a perfect place for the president to hold this reception (Fig. 21.2). This is the best time I've ever had and I cannot wait to be invited to another presidential reception. So long as I never open my mouth at a Board meeting, I'm sure to get invited again. Cliff has already seen the menu for the next presidential reception. The entree is my absolute favorite--fresh Louisiana catfish. It will be the first harvest of catfish from State U.'s brand new Culpepper Aquaculture Facility built by Colonel Culpepper over a decommissioned smelly old landfill.

The End

APPENDIX

Here are some more of Cliff's examples of Type I problems.

1. The university director of technology transfer signs a contract obligating a professor to do specific research for a corporation. The director does this without checking to see if the professor wants to do this research, if he has facilities to do the research, or if he can deliver on the contract in the specified time. The director completes the transaction in secret without the professor's knowledge or permission. When the professor cannot deliver on the contract, the company files a lawsuit against the professor. No administrator takes responsibility for the debacle. The professor is left to dangle in court.

2. From the president on down, top-level State U. administrators illegally recruit a nasty, dictatorial person to become chairman of a department. With the blessings of the administration, the despot usurps power from his democratically-elected predecessor. In effecting the coup, the State U. president and his cronies violate all relevant affirmative action regulations and written university policies. After nearly a year, when he is no longer able to suppress the grass-roots call for democracy, the co-conspiring Dean of Arts and Sciences caves in to faculty pressure and finally permits

the professors to vote (after the fact) on the new chairman (as required by his own college bylaws). But just before he allows the election to occur, the dean illegally transfers three outside professors into the department to stack the vote in the current chairman's favor. Some professors catch the dean red-handed in this illegal act of ballot box stuffing, but the president of State U. does nothing to remedy the situation. Instead he targets, for subsequent punishment, those professors who registered the complaint about the Dean of Arts and Sciences. A decade later, this same ballot-box-stuffing Dean of Arts & Sciences is chosen to be State U's president, at double the salary of his predecessor.

3. Several professors object, via prescribed channels, to their department chair's misuse of power and his violation of numerous written university policies. When junior administrators sidestep all possible forms of redress or adjudication, the professors appeal to the president. The president immediately retaliates. He arranges for the professors to be tried in absentia in a Star Chamber-type kangaroo court (appointed from the PPBR Panel). The president never provides the professors an opportunity for self-defense. The result of this inquisition is the eviction of three professors from their departments. Eviction notices, effective at the moment of receipt, are delivered by armed university plainclothesmen. The case dies in court after seven years of lawyer procrastination and incompetent handling of the case by the AAUP (the faculty union).

4. In a letter over his signature, the president of State U. awards merit pay increases to 789 professors. While promising a salary increase, the president's letter fails to specify the dollar amount of each award. Immediately after the letters are mailed, a lesser assistant administrator in the Office of Personnel realizes he misread the electronic files sent to him by the Office of the Provost. Of the 789 professors notified, only 505 had made the provost's final cut. The other 284 were below the cutoff line and not slated for merit pay. The president chooses not to honor his promise to the 284 "misinformed" professors, even though he could have divided the appropriated pool of merit pay dollars 789 ways instead of 505 ways. Nobody would have been the wiser. But instead of taking personal responsibility for the debacle, as any honorable person might, the president orders the lesser assistant administrator to take the rap. He makes the lesser assistant administrator write each of the 284 professors

himself, assuming personal responsibility for the "terrible mistake." The president awards the lesser assistant administrator a huge merit pay increase in the next round as payoff for his taking the rap for the president's debacle.

5. Renovations of a molecular biology building are so poorly planned and so poorly executed by the Facilities and Maintenance administrators that (1) none of the newly installed, ghastly expensive windows works, (2) power spraying of the building soaks a bench full of computers (because the new windows won't close), (3) mounds of dust are delivered to every square inch of the building for half a year, postponing or ruining countless experiments, (4) fume hoods are turned off for a week contaminating the building with carcinogens and other toxic chemicals, and (5) refrigerators and freezers are shut down for fourteen hours, ruining millions of dollars worth of frozen biological materials.

    An elaborate electrical switchover plan was to have kept the department's dozens of refrigerators and freezers continuously powered throughout the electrical renovations. The scheme cost $60,000 — yet the plan failed miserably. Administrators responsible for the debacle deny all responsibility. Instead, they cover their own personal posteriors adhering to the PPPP policy (see Chapter 18). They irresponsibly blame the professors for not having moved (during finals week) hundreds of thousands of valuable samples to other non-existing freezers and other non-existing refrigerators. The department chairman undermines the professors in his own department by repeatedly congratulating the construction supervisors for work well done. This is how department chairs get promoted — by screwing over their own faculty while appeasing high level administrators.

6. Tensions between faculty and the State U. president escalate over countless issues of administration mismanagement. A professor publicly appeals to the Governing Board for an ombudsman to help solve faculty-administration disputes, especially those involving the president. Instead of appointing an ombudsman, instead of studying the issue, instead of working on a solution, the chairman of the Governing Board orders the university internal auditor to participate in an intelligence-gathering and retaliatory sting operation against professors who have raised the ombudsman issue. Eight courageous and trusting professors take the bait.

Unbeknownst to the professors, the chairman of the Governing Board, the internal auditor, and the president are all conspiring in an illegal act of entrapment. Following the internal auditor's intelligence-gathering activities (private, confidential interviews with each of the eight professors), the president delivers severe punishment to the now entrapped professors. The fact that entrapment followed by punishment is a felony is of no concern to the conspiring administrators. No reporter investigates the story. No state official or U.S. Congressman, fully apprised of the situation, responds (no votes to be gained in this situation). The mess is held up in court for nearly a decade as the faculty union (the AAUP) ineptly blows all aspects of the case. The plaintiffs give up all hope of justice. The auditor gets promoted. The president gets reappointed with a huge salary increase.

7. Based upon his long-standing and unique pre-eminence in biotechnology research and teaching, a professor lands an industrial contract worth $500,000. State U. regulations require the director of technology transfer to be the official contract signatory. The director signs this contract. The professor complies with every provision of the contract and then, beyond the scope of the contract, voluntarily spends $20,000 of his own research money to help promote the company's product. Despite the professor's 100 percent compliance with every contract provision, the company fails to make payment. By State U. regulations, the professor is prevented from enforcing collection on his own. It is the specific responsibility of technology transfer and the Vice-President of Research to collect delinquent payments from companies under contract with State U. Six years go by and the company makes no payments. Over the six-year period, the professor appeals to the State U. administration to enforce the contract. The administration refuses to do so and refuses to answer the professor's letters. In an apparent attempt to justify their six-year-long pattern of concerted neglect in this matter, administrators manufacture one flimsy, disingenuous excuse after another. They concoct their ludicrous stories to keep from having to admit responsibility for past or present administration failures. Throughout the affair, dozens of administrators and lackey-lawyers circle the wagons in steadfast refusal to do anything productive. They fritter away hundreds and hundreds of hours with administration stonewalling and denials. The money is never collected. The professor's research program is seriously crippled and he is

tied up in meaningless and futile litigation for years to follow. Then, to rub salt into the wounds they've inflicted, administrators deny the professor's applications for promotion on grounds that he has failed to bring in sufficient outside money.

8. In a "Saturday Night Massacre," The president of State U. eliminates the entire office of the Provost (one hundred employees) in order to escape a faculty initiative to hold public hearings on his competence in office.

9. An Hispanic female professor of Romance Languages is denied promotion and tenure. She initiates a grievance against the administration, alleging discrimination on the basis of gender and national origin. She has a strong case and it is clear to all involved that she will win a unanimous grievance decision. To protect their guilty cronies, the administration suspends the grievance unilaterally, violating all relevant university policies and its contract with the faculty in the process. The administration continues their delaying tactics until the Hispanic female professor's probationary year expires. Now her fight against university discrimination is exacerbated by her having to wage battle from a distant state. The burden is too great for her. So, having beaten down the will of an otherwise energetic professor, the State U. administration wins the grievance on a trivial technicality.

INDEX

Abstinence, Assoc. Dean of Sexual, 36
Alaska, baked, 189
Amazons, 36, 38
Amelican correge, 29, 30
Axe (a good way to pose a question), 19, 20, 22
Axe (the kind for chopping alligator tails), 19
Axes (the kind for chopping wood), 104
Axes (the kind for graphs), 20, 104, 106
Beer, 1, 2, 6, 18, 47, 73, 167, 186
Beheadings, public, 144
Bellybutton jewelry, 41
Buff, the, 45
Cheerleaders, butt naked, 174
Chewing gum in high school, 36
Circumcision, Pomp And, 137
Cleveland, 82
Clinton, Chelsea, 11
Clothes, the emperor has no, 122
Cows, 35
Cuffs, 41
Custodian, 101, 149
D, 128, 143
D, Ph, x, 98
Diseases, foot-related sexually transmitted, 115
DNA, 22
Doofus, flat-out, 181
Drawer, sock, 46
Ear removal, 41
Earth, salt of the, 73, 74
Embellish, 122, 145, 146
English sheep dog, 41
Enrichment, noun-adjective, 66
Exchange, stock, 34, 35

Executions, public, 144
Fart, royal, 84, 85
Fish, cat, 12, 42, 43, 136, 139, 152, 157, 193
Fish, swallowing slithering fin, 45
Ft. Lauderdale, 45
Garfunkel, Simon and, 37
Food, real good, 183
Gown, 133, 135, 136
Gown, flimsy, 133, 136
Gown, see-through paper, 133
Hippies, 37
Inseams, 41
Jupiter, 38
Keep it in your pants, 3
Kong, Hong, 128
Kvestion, 55
Matter, vii, ix, 17, 49, 53, 83, 85, 91, 95, 106, 120, 149, 150, 155, 181, 186, 198
Mauve, 3
My!, Oh, 3
National Weather Service, 4
Ni, tai ni po, 29
Note, tiny pink, 52
November 29, 10
Ocean blue, 86
Ohio, 3
One nanopoint, 84
Pat Boone, 37
Parentis, in loco, 35, 37, 43
Phrenology, 43, 126
Plane, air, viii, 42
Plane, the inclined, 73
Plato, 121
Plobrem, 27
Pockets, ix, 146
Porn, peddling Granddad's, 43, 45

Pushers, pedal, 41
Quietly quacking, 5
Quiz, 100 point trial, 114
Real big thing, 36
Real good, xi, xii, 1, 4, 6, 7, 9, 12, 13, 15, 16, 17, 20, 23, 48, 63, 66, 68, 69, 71-4, 77, 78, 80, 86, 88, 95, 96, 98, 100, 101, 103, 104, 109, 111, 117, 120, 123, 124, 125, 128, 137, 143, 144, 152, 153, 155, 157, 162, 164, 167, 169, 170, 172, 176, 182, 183, 189
Rutgers, 43
Ruth, Babe, 5, 59
Salmonella surprise, 54
Sewer pipe, 51, 92, 149, 171
Sex, 39, 44, 45, 47, 53, 55, 173
Sex, all day I dream about, 39
Sheep dog, 41
Sheepskin, 60, 83
Speling, vii, xii, 6, 17, 18, 21, 22, 61, 62, 63, 70, 136
Syzygy, 72
Szalay, Mr, 63
Tarts, Pop, 13, 14, 24, 84
Testosterone, 36
Times, it was the best of, 78
Times, it was the worst of, 78
Tsunamis, 135
U, Stata, 34, 144
U, State, vii, x, xi, xii, 2, 3, 5, 7, 9, 11, 12, 14, 22, 24, 26-9, 33-6, 38, 39, 41, 43-6, 48, 49, 50, 53, 54, 55, 59, 61, 67, 68, 73, 76, 79, 81, 83, 84, 87, 88, 90, 96, 100, 115, 118-21, 126, 128, 130, 132, 136-39, 143-65, 167, 169-74, 177, 178, 180-91, 193, 195-99
UPCA, 26
Vice-neutron, assistants to the, 147
Wagon, Conestoga, 46
Wood shop, 13, 14, 24
Zeppelin, 103
Zybylbd Bvlspzk, 126
Zyrian, 122

www.ingramcontent.com/pod-product-compliance
Lightning Source LLC
Chambersburg PA
CBHW080501110426
42742CB00017B/2966